ALASTAIR NIVEN has had a distinguished career as a writer, lecturer and administrator. He was director of literature at the Arts Council and at the British Council and is a former president of English PEN. A special interest in Africa and the Commonwealth dates from his university years. He is married and lives in London.

KRISTIN HEADLAM painted the portrait of the author on the cover of this book, photographed by Alex Niven. An award winning Australian artist, Headlam's work may be found in many collections, including the British Museum and the National Gallery of Australia.

IN GLAD OR SORRY HOURS

a memoir
by

Alastair Niven

©2021 Alastair Niven
ISBN 0-936315-48-2
STARHAVEN, 42 Frognal, London NW3 6AG
books@starhaven.org.uk
https://www.facebook.com/starhaven.org.uk/

Typeset in Palatino Linotype

CONTENTS:

Take now, my boy, this book of song:
My say is brief – may yours be long!
Only, in glad or sorry hours,
Culling this field of Fancy's flowers
Perhaps you'll drop, when I am gone
One little flower on me, my son.

– Alexander Mair, 'To C.G.R.Mair'

1

ORIGINS: SCOTLAND, 1940s

According to my mother I should have been the King of Scotland. I might have to bide my time and there would be the small problem in a land of primogeniture of having two elder brothers. She was fairly sure, though, that if Robert the Bruce had not slaughtered the Red Comyn in 1306 the royal succession would have come down to us. I never fully understood this because she had six surviving brothers, five of whom had children, as well as an elder sister with three sons. By coincidence the family she had married into had Cummings, presumably a corruption of Comyn, as a family name. I worked out by the time I was a teenager, spending many an hour poring over genealogical spreads of every dynasty in Europe, that if there was any question of my inheriting the crown through the

Comyn lineage it was more likely because of my father than my mother. That did not deter her. Indeed, she made it clear throughout their bumpy marriage of over 57 years that she had done my father a favour by condescending to wed him. 'Your father's grandfather was a butcher in Dundee' was one of her favourite lines, always ensuring that all who heard it knew she was a professor's daughter.

My father was without snobbery. Alas, he was without wit as well and no match for her rather brilliant tongue. He was the one with a degree from Cambridge – well, just: he got an Ordinary pass rather than the honors for which he had sat. She had no formal education after she left St. Margaret's Ladies College in Edinburgh at the age of eighteen. She had, however, three qualities which no amount of learning can bestow. She was warm with people. She was intuitively intelligent. She was beautiful, her creamy complexion lasting her whole life and her black hair slipping only slowly into silvertude. Her name for formal purposes such as signing cheques, which she could rarely afford to do, or appearing on electoral rolls, when she could be relied on to vote Conservative, was Elizabeth Isobel Robertson Mair. Elizabeth and Isobel are really the same name, but as my grandfather had six daughters and seven sons he could not always be expected to be on top of appellations. He registered Hildegarde as the middle name of two of his daughters. My mother was always known as Betty. She was the second of thirteen. Her sisters were Katie, Eileen, Enid, Gwen and Rosaleen, and her brothers were Gilbert, Alastair, Kenneth, Leslie, Colin, Hugh and Norman. Hugh died of meningitis when just a month old, but all the others lived to adulthood and in most cases to a great age.

I have always been proud of my grandfathers, though I knew neither of them. Professor Alexander Mair died in 1928 in a fire and Ernest Niven C.I.E. died of a cerebral haemorrhage in 1932, only weeks after he had retired from the post of Chief Civil Engineer to the port of Rangoon. For two lads from Scotland to achieve such heights must say something about the excellence of the educational grounding they received.

Alexander Mair – or Alec as he was always called – came from Keith, a small town in Banffshire. His father, another Alexander, became in 1899 the last Moderator of the United Presbyterian Church of Scotland. When Alec was fourteen he went to Aberdeen University and at seventeen he was a student at Cambridge. Ten years later, in 1908, he was appointed Professor of Greek at Edinburgh University, where he remained until his death. He occupied his chair for twenty-three years and, along with his friend Gilbert Murray, was regarded as the best classicist in the country. He was famed for devotion to his students, many of whom, like the runner Eric Liddell, came regularly to Sunday lunch.

I have only the dimmest recollections of my maternal grandmother, for she died when I was five, but she must have been remarkable to survive seventeen pregnancies, give birth to thirteen healthy children, and become renowned for her hospitality. Her youngest child,

Norman, was only three weeks old when her husband died in 1928. He was working in his study one November night and appears to have fallen asleep, no doubt over a dram or two of whisky, there being a liking of too much alcohol which still runs in the family. My father and mother were in the house at the time, because my father used to board with the Mairs while his own parents were overseas, and when the fire was discovered they climbed out of their bedrooms down knotted sheets. On the pavement outside the fire officer asked my grandmother if she could account for everyone in the house, including her twelve surviving children, and she said she could. Then a thought occurred to her. 'Oh! The professor isn't here'. He was discovered dead, slumped over a Greek text. My father told me that he had seen the burned body, completely destroyed down the right side but intact on the left. To his delight he located a ten-shilling note in my grandfather's breast pocket, 'absolutely unblemished and ready to spend'.

Hesiod, Callimachus, Lycophron and Pindar were Grandfather Mair's classical specialisms. At Aberdeen University and then at Cambridge he scooped every academic distinction and prize open to him. It was, though, as a teacher and a poet that he shone brightest.

He took infinite pains to know his students both in his ordinary and his honours classes, and if he saw anyone struggling in difficulties he would invite him out to his house and go over his work with him like an ordinary tutor. He and his wife extended boundless hospitality to the students, who made free of their home and the expansive meals provided for them. During the vacations they always had students staying with them. If when Mair died he was in financial difficulties, it was in no small measure because of the lavish entertainment he had provided for a generation of undergraduates, many of the poorer ones finding in his home the only private house in Edinburgh they ever entered during the whole of their University course. (1)

My mother's natural generosity towards young people, and the fact that our home when growing up became something of a refuge for our friends with less hospitable parents, was clearly derived from the environment in which she was reared. My own love of literature may have had its genetic origin in my grandfather's intuitive passion for good poetry. H. J. C. Grierson, who was Knight Professor of English Literature at the University of Edinburgh at the time of my grandfather's death and is chiefly remembered today as rescuer of the then nearly forgotten Metaphysical poets, wrote of him 'Many can discourse on the subject-matter of a poet, his "criticism of life". Few can illuminate the poet's art with insight and discrimination. Mair did...' (2) His poetry acknowledges many sources and some of his poems were versions of masters he admired: Horace, Martial, Heine, Tennyson. He was as agile in Scots as he was in classical English and he delighted in translating into impeccable Greek such standard anthologised works as 'Crossing the Bar' and 'Clementine'. At my mother's funeral in 1993 I just about managed to get through a reading of his 'Song Before Sunrise'.

On my dim life a little while there strayed
A beam of light:
It was thy coming, O my love, which made

The darkness bright.
More wert thou to me than the Heaven's sweet rain
    To flowers that bloom:
But lo! The light is gone and I again
    Am wrapt in gloom.
As children sitting in a darkened house
    Drear hours and long,
To cheer their heavy hearts will sometimes rouse
    A childish song,
So I, a foolish child, in darkness sit
    And sing to thee,
And though it rings a little sadly, yet
    It comforts me.' (3)

My other grandfather grew up as the son of a butcher in the 'juteopolis' city of Dundee and spent much of his working life in Burma. Young Ernest understood the importance of being noticed. When he was fifteen, an engineer by the name of George Buchanan took him under his wing and gave him basic training in engineering. It was possible in the early decades of the last century to become a civil engineer without passing an examination. Apprenticed to Buchanan, he accompanied him to Burma, then a part of India, when his master took a senior post in Rangoon. He advanced quickly and remained with Buchanan off and on for twenty years. Together they were deployed in Mesopotamia in 1915, clearing pollution and designing wharves, weirs and landing stages for the Shatt-Al-Arab and Basra waterways. Later Buchanan, an irascible egotist, fell out with his employers and was expelled from the British

Institute of Civil Engineers, though not before he had been knighted for his work in what is now Iraq.

Ernest had a two-year spell in London from 1917 to 1919, returning to England on a ship which was torpedoed just off Marseilles. My father, seven years old at the time, remembered this well and told me how he and his tiny sister Mabel had been taken to the shore in a lifeboat, with no sign of Raymond, his younger brother by just a year. It turned out that the little boy had been rescued and was on a different boat. The family was re-united in France and completed their journey to England by train. Mabel had been born at Monkey Point in Burma on my father's fifth birthday. Some unwise elder announced that she was my father's birthday present, whereupon Raymond asked why he hadn't been given a baby for his birthday.

Ernest's role in London was as Director of the National Ordnance Factories and Director of Ordnance Supplies at the Ministry of Munitions. These were wartime posts and, on their completion, he returned to Rangoon where, within two years, he was appointed to his prestigious Chief Civil Engineer position. He left my father behind, facing years at boarding schools, first and briefly in Dover and latterly for the whole of his secondary education at Fettes College in Edinburgh. His parents came home by ship every five years, so after the age of nine my father only saw them together at the ages of twelve, seventeen, and finally twenty-two. Ernest took early retirement from Rangoon in 1932. He died unexpectedly in London the same year, his haemorrhage the consequence of a brain tumour.

His widow Clara initially moved back to Scotland, then settled in Bath for part of the war years, in the same street as Emperor Haile Selassie of Ethiopia, with whom she used to walk in the morning as they exercised their dogs. After the war she bought a house in Shortlands, near Bromley in Kent, and it was there that I used mainly to visit her. She was a strait-laced Scotswoman, probably less disapproving than she came across. I loved her house, which was full of mementoes of her time in Burma, and she let me play with the contents of 'the cabinet' – a mounted ostrich's egg, small knives of lethal sharpness, ceramic Buddhas and, my favourite, which I still have, a six-foot long beaded snake made by a Turkish prisoner of war in Mesopotamia in 1917. My mother and her mother-in-law did not get on. Though completely skint through all the years they knew each other, my mother was regarded as extravagant by the Niven side of the family. As a result, Grannie Niven, as we called her, rarely visited us. Her Christmas gift to my mother was usually a dish cloth or kitchen towel. It was only in my teens that I began to perceive that she was rather lonely. I tried to make amends by occasionally cutting her grass, but she had a gift for making one feel one might have suggested the wrong thing. One gloriously hot July afternoon with clear blue skies I rang her to propose coming over to do a bit of gardening. 'Oh, I don't think you should, Alastair. It's coming over all black,' the A's in 'Alastair' and 'black' drawn out and heightened as in the word 'dark'. That spoke for her view of the world.

My father, Harold, was a bit of a playboy as a young man. He spent as much time as he could enjoying cross country running, rugger and particularly golf, which at his best he played to a handicap of four. He ran a sports car when he was only eighteen. He went briefly to Edinburgh University, then to Cambridge, but he hit the buffers with a jolt on realizing that life with well-to-do parents funding his lifestyle from overseas had come to an abrupt end with his father's death. He was by then an officer in the Argyll and Sutherland Highlanders, based at Stirling Castle. It was impossible in the early 1930s to maintain such a life on an army salary alone. Unfortunately, my grandfather's will had stipulated that money should only pass to his children on the death of my grandmother, which did not happen for another thirty-eight years. My father had thus to find an alternative to the military career he had envisaged. After unsuccessful interviews with many well-known companies like Wills Tobacco, which came about through his posh public school connections, he joined the City of London police, part of its fast track recruitment of graduates in the mid-1930s.

My mother had thought when she married in 1935 that she was embarking on a life as an army officer's spouse. She never reconciled herself to being a policeman's wife. Perhaps their marriage was doomed from the start, bored almost before the banns were called because they had known each other from childhood. Living alongside one another in school vacations, they grew into their teens and early adulthood almost as if brother and sister. My father's best friends were my mother's older siblings and among hers were his schoolmates. After their wedding in Edinburgh, however, she was wrenched from her familiar and familial world to a rented flat in Holloway, north London. It was dreary, their income was poor, and she knew very few people. When their first child, my brother Peter, arrived in 1938 she had to pull a pram up several flights of stairs every time she came back in after shopping.

They each had a good war, but separately. By the time it broke out in 1939 they had acquired a pleasant semi-detached house in Acland Crescent, just off Denmark Hill in south London. It was part of a new development on a former landed estate and had a large garden with a tall monkey puzzle tree around whose sinister shapes and gaunt black foliage I was in later years to weave many a private tale. There were damson and plum trees from an older orchard and a steep rockery leading down to an expanse of grass big enough to play abbreviated forms of cricket and tennis. One night in 1940 a bomb fell a few houses up the road, killing the family inside. My mother decided instantly to leave London. She scooped up her son and took the night train to Edinburgh to stay with her mother.

There followed eight years of disruption and later of illness which perhaps no marriage could have withstood. Mother moved around, staying with friends or in rented accommodation until after the war, whilst my father lived largely in police quarters in the City of London. Their house was let fully furnished – to Germans! Their tenants' contribution to the war effort was to let the grass grow as high as an elephant's eye, smash every one of my parents' wedding presents, and bunk off without settling their final debts. My mother, in blissful ignorance of what was happening in London, moved from Edinburgh to Silloth on the Solway firth, scene of many of her family's holidays from 1910 onwards. Some RAF officers based nearby ensured that there was a reasonable social life. Later in the war she moved to Chiddingfold in Surrey and thence to Ketton in Rutland, where they stayed as guests of their friends Donald and Marie Soper. The best-known Methodist preacher in the country, Soper was an exacting host and would reprimand my mother if she so much as raised her voice at her recalcitrant two-year old. Peter was baptised by him under the kitchen tap, starting a tradition, for we were all christened at home and, nonconformist style, without Godparents.

Father had a matey time in police accommodation at Snow Hill, playing golf whenever he could and from time to time fulfilling his uxorial duties by spending a few days wherever my mother was currently based. Colin was one result, born in 1941, and I another. I came into the world at 4.55 a.m. on Friday 25th February 1944. Mother retuned to Edinburgh for these births. As she entered the nursing home in Grosvenor Street, Haymarket, to have me, a bird shat on her head. Normally a sign of good fortune, she took one look at me and decided that this item of folklore was not infallible.

I was called Alastair after her brother who had been born on the 29th February, the leap day on which I had been expected. I was sometimes called Sandy in my early years, just as my own son Alexander was to be known until he rebelled after seeing the film *Grease*, where Sandy is a girl. My middle names are Neil, simply because Grannie Niven liked the name, and Robertson, with which all the Mair siblings and most of their offspring were endowed. Coincidentally my father was Harold Robertson Niven, acquiring the Robertson from his mother's maiden name. Shortly after my arrival, Mother moved to Moffatt in the Borders and there I began to be a sentient being.

2

SCHOOLS: LONDON, 1950s and 1960s

We were only a few months in Moffatt before the war ended. My earliest memory is of sitting on my grandmother's knee in a kitchen in Edinburgh. There is a dark green dresser, a large black range, and a cauldron hanging from a chimney breast in which the week's supply of porridge has been prepared on the previous Sunday night. Grannie Mair looks tired. Her grey hair, crinkled brow and puffy cheeks make her seem quite vulnerable. It is no surprise when five years later, still only in her sixties, she quietly dies after having contracted a winter virus. By that stage we are back in London. The phone rings with the news. It is four days before Christmas. Mother comes off the 'phone and quietly tells us 'Grannie has died!'. I don't fully understand what has happened but when I learn that of the twelve surviving siblings, she is the only one not able to attend her mother's snowy funeral on Boxing Day 1951, I feel an anger and grief for her which has never been assuaged. My father had little money, but he could afford his golfing trips and the new shirt he would give himself every Christmas. Surely it would have been possible to find a return train fare to Edinburgh. My mother said little about it, but the wound never healed. I mark that moment as the point of no return in their relationship.

I have always assumed that cancer could be occasioned by stress. The term was not much used in the 1940s, but years of caring alone for three small boys, of upheavals and separations, and of finally returning to a part of London where she was surrounded by bomb sites and found her own home denuded and blighted, took its toll on my mother's health. She was diagnosed with breast cancer in 1947, a year notable for one of the severest winters on record. Colin fell ill with nephritis and about the same time Peter contracted scarlet fever and had to be isolated from the rest of us for several weeks. I was to learn many years later that our mother had a fourth pregnancy at this time, a girl, my never-to-be sister. Perhaps she would have been called Sally or Lydia, two names I was told were under consideration for me until I arrived under the wrong label. I came across a letter written shortly after my birth from my mother in Edinburgh to my father in London in which there is thinly disguised disappointment that I was not a girl, but assurance that the doctors said there was plenty of scope for another go. It never happened. The pregnancy was aborted because of the cancer.

Mother spent the best part of two years in and out of King's College Hospital in London and the Royal Infirmary in Edinburgh. Through one of her brother-in-law's connections, she had top notch attention, with her operations conducted by perhaps the two most prominent surgeons in the country, Sir John Peel and Sir John Bruce. My father was told at one stage that the outlook was grim and that it was unlikely that she would survive more than six months. He was wondering what to do when left with three boys under the age of ten. Cancer diagnosis was much less precise than it is today, so perhaps her determination to live was not as miraculous as it must have seemed at the time.

Most of the pathos and drama of what was going on passed me by. After a period with our grandmother in Edinburgh, Peter was sent to live with some London friends, 'Kem' and Dorothea Kemble in Herne Hill. Colin and I were packed off to Hucknall in Nottinghamshire where my mother's elder sister Katie lived with her doctor husband, Ronnie Vartan. It was a magical time for us. The house was large, their own sons were away at boarding school so supplied no competition, and we had access to their tennis court and toys. The only downside was a requirement to sit under a sun ray lamp for twenty minutes every day and then take a long siesta after lunch. This was chronically boring. It was not therefore surprising that Colin tried to murder me, more for something to do than because I was an annoying little wretch. 'Do you see that thing on the skirting board with two holes in it? Why not lick your fingers and put them on the holes and I'll turn on the switch next to them?' I reeled across the room but survived. Looking back my life was more at risk from our strict aunt. When Colin and I, who were always bathed together before bedtime, decided one evening to have a peeing competition in the bath, we went without supplies for the whole of the next day.

On my fourth birthday a cake was made and candles lit. One of them keeled over and set fire to the paper frill. That was just about the most exciting event of the months we spent apart from our parents. Eventually we returned to London, to the same house the family had bought before the war. Mother came out of hospital and, apart from her regular check-ups, never referred again to her illness. One day, however, I stumbled into her bedroom while she was dressing. She was facing a mirror and in it I could see her scarred front. Even then I knew that women were supposed to have two breasts. She had only one and in place of the other was a wrinkled flatness. I kept the information to myself and often wondered if I had imagined what I had seen, but there was the evidence of the cotton wool padding she pinned into her bras and sometimes left dangling on a chair.

Peter was sent away to boarding school while Mother was ill. Dulwich College was only a couple of miles from where we lived, but with her out of action it was convenient for him to live at the school whilst Colin and I were being looked after elsewhere. He so loved the life that he stayed on as a boarder throughout his school career. Colin and I meanwhile, on returning to London, went to Dulwich Hamlet Primary School. It was an early example of our mother's determination to ensure that we had the best education available. She instinctively knew that this was more likely at a feeder school to the local independents, Dulwich College, Alleyn's School and James Allen's Girls' School, than at the physically nearer Bessemer Grange Primary. She blagged our way into Dulwich Hamlet with some tale of how we needed to be near our absentee brother. It was a shrewd move because as a result we had an outstanding educational start to life.

My memories of Dulwich Hamlet are very warm, but also vague. My thrill at showing off must have been endemic because all my memories of the time pertain to performance. I recall reciting Hilaire Belloc's 'Rebecca' to a goggle-eyed class of children who, wickedly, had not bothered to learn a whole poem. The moral of Belloc's tale of punishment for the little girl who slammed doors was clearly transferable to all situations of not doing as one was told, learning poems included:

> Her funeral Sermon (which was long
> And followed by a sacred song)
> Mentioned her Virtues, it is true

But dwelt upon her Vices too,
And showed the Dreadful End of One
Who goes and slams the door for fun. (4)

We had an annual May Festival and I was cast as the May Queen's page of honour. How I adored Susan Hathaway for at least a week. I was dressed in a black tunic with black breeches and a white lace *jabot*.

I present to you your new May Queen.
I pray you be as kind to her as you to me have been.

I was Joseph in the Nativity Play, a non-speaking role. I remember an uncle telling me of the revolting child who in the same part had stepped forward to announce of the baby in the crib, 'It's a girl!' I was so tempted to do the same.

And then there was the death of the King. On 6th February 1952 we were gathered in the school hall for a dance class, which we performed to music on the radio. Suddenly the programme was interrupted. A solemn voice made an announcement on air. I had no idea what it meant, but the head teacher, Miss Barnes, then called the whole school into an assembly and, in words that made sense to a seven year old, told us that His Majesty had died and we now had a Queen. It is extraordinary looking back at that moment to recall how every parent was contacted by telephone and asked to come at once to pick up their child or children, as the school would of course be closed as a sign of respect. Within half an hour our mother had arrived to take

Colin and me home. Even then there must have been some mothers who went out to work, to say nothing of many working fathers, and some kind of provision must have been made for them in the ensuing closure, but the norm was one (female) parent at home while the other (male) went to the office.

A few months later my mother came into my bedroom and as she drew the curtains told me 'Queen Mary is dead'. These royal moments stand out as markers in one's childhood, no doubt underlying what a conventional family we were but also instilling in me a lasting conviction that monarchy has been the glue which binds British society. It has been an adventure to travel most of my life on a parallel pathway to the Queen's. On 2nd June 1953 these paths converged, as they did for many, in a suburban sitting room watching the Coronation. We were invited by Scottish friends of my parents, the Durnos, to follow the events on their television. I had never seen a television before and was rarely to do so again in my childhood or adolescence because it was believed to be a distraction from serious matters like school homework. It was not until after I had completed my last 'A' level exam eleven years later that we acquired a television. My father, having railed against the idea, now became an addict and from that day to the end of his life it was seldom off.

We lived a quiet life in our semi-detached house. Under no circumstances were we permitted to play in the street. That was what 'common' children did. We had friends, though, and even a couple of celebrity neighbours. The boxer Freddie Mills, former world light heavyweight champion, lived just round the corner and we were friendly with his stepson Don. Next door was the bandleader Johnny Douglas, best remembered now for having composed the soundtrack to the film *The Railway Children*. One evening he asked me in to meet Vera Lynn and her husband Harry Lewis. I was about eleven and awestruck, especially by their Rolls Royce parked outside. The singer not only gave me a signed photograph, with 'Sincerely Yours, Vera Lynn' scrawled across it, but several test records, 78 r.p.m. vinyl discs with recordings of unreleased songs on only one side. Johnny and his wife Irene frequently had blazing rows, largely conducted in the open air. Colin and I would sit at a bedroom window, as though we were at Centre Court in Wimbledon, watching the plates they threw at each other wing their way from left to right. And then there was Charlie Richardson, who lived further down our road. One evening he knocked at the door, collecting money for charity. 'I don't know what's come over Charlie!' said my father. 'That was so unlike him.' The next day we read of his arrest. A violent gangster, specialising in torture, he had perhaps been repenting of his sins at the twelfth hour.

In 1954 I passed the entrance examination for Dulwich College and joined my brothers, Colin having preceded me as a day boy. Both Peter and Colin were good at games, especially rugby and hockey. I was not, though in time, mainly because I stayed on at school until I was 19, it was I and not either of them who ended up as captain of our athletic house. It was strange seeing my eldest brother, now a senior prefect, captain of his boarding house and a sporting hero as fullback for the First Fifteen, in an entirely different context from the vacation weeks when he was at home. He regarded me as a mild form of pestilence and did everything to avoid me, especially when he was taking a detention one day and I kept pressing my face against the window, waggling my ears and sticking out my tongue. Colin meanwhile soared to the top, becoming in time school captain as well as a big fish in the school army cadet force – something I was cajoled into joining as an alternative to being a scout, but heartily loathed. I was not well co-ordinated, so presenting arms with one of the First World War rifles which were issued to us was a form of purgatory. Worse was the embarrassingly heavy khaki uniform we had to wear once a week, complete with army gaiters and heavy belt.

I had a bad start to life at Dulwich because I was simply not good at much. I was nearly a year younger than the others in my class and hid behind that fact as a justification for regularly coming 29th or 30th in every subject out of a total of thirty. After two years I was kept back and obliged to repeat the year, now almost the oldest person in the class rather than youngest. I realised that I could write and speak with a certain amount of assurance and so started to do quite well in English and history. I struggled manfully with Latin, but otherwise I remained academically useless.

I made up for my lack of lustre in the classroom by becoming a committed member of the debating society. My confidence was boosted when I was asked to deliver the vote of thanks to Clement Attlee when he came to give a talk to the sixth form. He was well over 80 by then and inaudible to all but the front row, in which fortunately I was seated. I practised my speech until I was so word perfect that I can remember it to this day. It began 'The thanks we give to you, sir, are in sincere appreciation of the honour you have given us', delivered as though I was a town crier.

In time I did sufficiently well in inter-school competitions to be elected Chairman of the Public Schools Debating Association, presiding in 1961 over the annual *Observer* Mace, which in that year was won by a team from my own school. We had brilliant judges for the competition: journalist Kenneth Harris, who had been with the competition from its inception and who had written a classic account of juvenile debating, *Travelling Tongues*, which recounted the story of a speaking tour he had led to America with fellow students Edward Boyle and Anthony Wedgwood Benn; Dame Peggy Ashcroft, the most outstanding British actress of her day who I had recently seen perform as the Duchess of Malfi and who I regarded as one step above divinity; the said Edward Boyle, now an eminent Conservative politician and later to become an outstanding Vice-Chancellor at my doctoral university, Leeds; and the Countess of Longford, whose great biography of Queen Victoria still lay three years in the future. I recall her arriving at the City of London School, where the competition and celebratory dinner were being held, asking if she could have access to a TV because her daughter Catherine was appearing. It was not as easy as it sounded, but it taught me that some unforeseen request would almost certainly attend any event I was organising. Presiding benevolently over the whole occasion was Lord Hailsham, patron of the Association and a Tory grandee of immense acumen and bluntness. I met him at other debates after this. I recall one in particular, held at St Paul's Girls' School, when I slipped off to the lavatory. Opening the door of an unlocked cubicle I found the noble lord fully splayed on the seat, clearly in mid business. 'Oh, I'm terribly sorry!' I exclaimed, 'I will wait'. His Lordship was unperturbed. 'That would probably be best,' he replied, 'otherwise it might give rise to public comment'.

Dulwich College at the time was a great school. It had been founded by the actor Edward Alleyn in 1619 for twelve poor scholars – an act of repentance perhaps for his rollicking life style before then. It was said that whilst rehearsing Christopher Marlowe's *Dr Faustus*, in which he created the title part, Alleyn had counted eight devils on stage in a scene that required only seven. One was clearly the real thing. Since 1945 the College had been the home of 'the Dulwich experiment' whereby 90% of the boys attending did so on scholarships awarded by the then London County Council. It was a venture designed and initiated by one of those great left-wing educators who managed both to undermine and to uphold established conventions. Christopher Gilkes believed fully in traditional public-school values – that Character is Sport, as George Eliot might have put it, and wisdom is gained through study and hard work. He only deviated from other independent head teachers at the time by insisting that every child should have the opportunity to share in these values if they had the aptitude to do so; family circumstances should never stand in the way. The seventeenth-century founder of Alleyn's College of God's Gift had intended the school to be for less advantaged children and the Education Act of 1944 had made possible a modern interpretation of this high-minded principle. Gilkes negotiated with the County Council a pioneering scheme to enable boys from homes where fee paying would have been out of the question to avail themselves of a brilliant education.

Brilliant it truly was. Still, after decades, I cannot believe my good fortune in coinciding with such a radical experiment. It eventually petered out in the 1970s because, with the rise of comprehensive education, it was felt that the College was creaming off the brightest boys in south London and environs. My parents could never have afforded to pay full fees for three boys, but the Dulwich scheme neatly covered the years 1948 to 1963 when there was always a young Niven to benefit from it. The only costs to find for any of us was money for school uniforms. As we did not run a car, own a television, or go abroad for holidays, this was manageable. The termly visit to the school commissariat to stock up on blazers and boaters for the summer, pinstriped trousers, black jackets and stiff detachable collars for winter, all served by the eponymously named Mr Belt, who had probably been there since Edward Alleyn's time, was always an adventure.

The teaching at Dulwich was remarkable. True scholars on the staff included Philip Vellacott, who had translated Euripides for Penguin; James Gibson – nicknamed 'Cathie' after a Scottish Olympic swimmer – who was a Thomas Hardy expert *par excellence*; and E. N. Williams, a specialist in eighteenth-century constitutional history. There were others less academically famous, but who were inspiring teachers: Laurie Jagger, for example, who used to ask us to pick the name of a capital city and define it in some surrealistic way unconnected with its reality. I decided that Singapore was a rare skin disease and Paris the collective noun for parsing verbs. There was an overtly gay group of arts teachers who led school trips abroad. I kicked up such a fuss with my mother – always my mother, never my father – about not having travelled overseas that, unbeknown to me, she persuaded one of her brothers to pay for me to go to Florence in 1960.

The school dramatic society was a lifeline for someone who did not excel at sport. I had seen my first Shakespeare play at Dulwich College even before I became a pupil there: *King John*. This influenced me years later when our English teacher gave us a choice between studying *King John* or *Hamlet* for 'A' level and the class clubbed together to choose the former, just in order to be contrary. How we regretted it! I took part in the inter-house drama competitions and one year was awarded the acting cup for my 'voice beautiful' performance as the Chorus in Vellacott's translation of the *Alcestis* of Euripides.

> Gods manifest themselves in many ways,
> Bring many matters to surprising ends.
> The things we thought would happen do not happen,
> Things unexpected the gods make possible. (5)

The high spot of this dramatic activity was a masterly production of *Twelfth Night*, directed by a young history teacher called David Henschel. It was exquisitely designed. My own contribution in the non-speaking role of Attendant Lord was not the making of the production, but Henschel's nuanced and sophisticated direction certainly was. I came to know the play intimately and can to this day recite most of it word for word. There were so many outstanding productions: *Richard II*, with the young Simon Brett, later an inventive crime writer, in the title role; *Hamlet* with Christopher Braden, son of the Canadian actors and television personalities Bernard Braden and Barbara Kelly, as the Prince ('Did you enjoy it, Mr Braden?' I asked on the last night; 'It was sure lit for radio' came the reply); *A Midsummer Night's Dream* with Giles Block, later voice director for the Globe Theatre, as Bottom (he had as a youngster been a poignant Arthur appealing for his eyes in *King John*); *Coriolanus*, magnificently pitching Braden as Aufidius opposite gravel-voiced Dick Alford as Caius

Martius. I was a gauche actor, but just being in the slip-stream of these events gave me incomparable pleasure.

At the same time as rehearsing school plays, I was involved with a company called the Rafter Players which a school friend Nick Young had started up in the attic of his home. Our first production was *Much Ado About Nothing*. I tended to be cast as nobly ineffective (Don Pedro, Orsino) or old (Capulet, Gonzalo), though I did have my star moment as Leontes in *The Winter's Tale*: 'Alastair's play!' splashed the headline in the *South London Press*.

> There may be in the cup
> A spider steep'd, and one may drink, depart,
> And yet partake no venom, for his knowledge
> Is not infected: but if one present
> The abhorr'd ingredient to his eye, make known
> How he hath drunk, he cracks his gorge, his sides,
> With violent hefts. I have drunk, and seen the spider. (6)

These and other magnificent lines in this most conflicted of Shakespeare's characters have stayed with me all my life. Others in the play have not, because I never fully learned the script. I had the speeches in the last act, when Leontes stands before the reviving Hermione, sewn into my splendid blue satin cloak, which I would wield with a flourish while I frantically scanned the next words I must utter.

We took some of these productions to Denmark, Finland and Russia. We stayed with local families. Sixty years later I remain in touch with the first such family, the Ringgaards of Norre Nissum Gymnasium, near Lemwig in northern Jutland. We behaved fairly badly in some of the places we visited. In Leningrad, for example, we put a bra round a statue of Lenin in the Museum of Atheism. We were not seen and so not arrested, but worse was our mockery of the almost certainly sincere attempts by some good citizens of the beautiful, though at the time neglected, city of Leningrad to make friends with us. Three or four of us were invited to the university to record passages of Dickens. This, it was explained, was so that they could have authentic British accents reading the English novelist most admired in Russia. In our cockiness, however, we were sure that this was an attempt to get modern voices recording impressions of how poverty-stricken London was today, full of orphanages, workhouses and brutal exploitation. Given a passage from *Oliver Twist* or *Hard Times* we read it with an artificial jollity as though it was a description of wealth and sunny uplands. I hope that today's scholars at the Saint Petersburg State University pore over these tapes and ponder on how stupid young people must have been in England in the 1960s not to understand the miserable humanity they were so distorting by their aural antics.

I was particularly mortified in Helsinki when I had to open our production of *Twelfth Night*, wearing a wig like a cocker spaniel's ears and sonorously booming out lines that I now realise call for wistfulness and lyricism.

> If music be the food of love, play on.
> Give me excess of it, that surfeiting

A fashionable audience had been attracted to the performance, perhaps because we claimed some tenuous link with the British Council. I truly believe they had come thinking we were a variant on the Royal Shakespeare Company, but my declamatory opening lines quickly disabused them. I could physically feel the temperature dropping. It was one of the most humiliating moments of my life.

I stayed part of the Rafter Players until 1967 when we made a film of *The Tempest* at Rinsey Cove in Cornwall. I was cast as Gonzalo, the venerable counsellor who speaks of his utopian hopes for humankind:

> I' th' commonwealth I would by contraries
> Execute all things, for no kind of traffic
> Would I admit. No name of magistrate.
> Letters should not be known. Riches, poverty.
> And use of service – none. Contract, succession,
> Bourn, bound of land, tilth, vineyard – none.
> No use of metal, corn or wine, or oil.
> No occupation: all men idle, all. (8)

These inspiringly socialist words have always stirred me. Years later, when giving a prestigious lecture on post-colonial literature at the Commonwealth Institute in London, I drew on them for the nexus of my argument. I called the lecture 'Gonzalo's Vision'. Our film was made in black and white and stands up well today, over fifty years on. By that time, however, I was living in Africa and I had to rush back there before the sound-track was dubbed. As a result, it carries my image as Gonzalo, but with the voice of a fellow member of the cast, Roger Sherman, speaking my words, in addition to portraying the drunken butler Stephano.

Our film of *The Tempest* lay well in the future, though the roots of it were in our attic rehearsals when still teenagers. School work dominated our lives far more than acting. Dulwich College at the time vied with Manchester Grammar School for winning the most scholarships each year to Oxford and Cambridge. I won an Open Exhibition in English to Cambridge in 1962 but was threatened with not being eligible to take it up because at the time a condition of entry was the acquisition of four core 'O' levels: in English literature, no problem; in a modern language, for which I mustered a pass in French; Latin, which I actually enjoyed; and mathematics or a science. No amount of attempts to pass maths worked and since I was permanently at war with my teacher in the subject, Jock Llewellyn, there was little prospect of me doing so. I tried physics and scored 7%, which is the mark awarded for being able to quote accurately Archimedes' Principle of fluid displacement. I wrote beautifully phrased appeals to my examiner at the end of each maths paper pointing out that my life would be forever blighted if he did not pass me. In desperation at seeing one of his precious award-ees slipping the net and possibly letting Manchester Grammar seize the crown that year, the Master of the College, Ronald Groves, who was a chemist, told me that he would provide one to one tuition in chemistry for the next two terms. It would mean staying on at the College beyond Christmas, but it paid dividends.

In stature Groves was a short man. My first day at the school back in 1954 had also been his first. As a new boy I went a day ahead for various introductory procedures. That evening on my return home my brothers grilled me as to what the new head was like. I was probably quite tall for eleven years, but they nevertheless listened with disbelief as I told them that he was shorter than me. He was, being possibly under five foot, and of course he remained so, but it did not stop him being a most intimidating man, especially when seated at his desk testing me on chemical equations. I passed the examination with a comfortable 56% and thus was able to follow my brothers to Cambridge, but it had been a close-run thing.

Dulwich was an inspiring school and many of my life-long friendships were formed there. Other friendships were ephemeral, but they helped to shape me. Though Chris Braden died young, his wit and ease of manner in the company of his celebrity parents taught me a lot about how to communicate informally with older people. I delighted too in the company of Michael Ondaatje, who passed briefly through Dulwich *en route* from Ceylon (not yet Sri Lanka) to Canada. As our class was organised alphabetically, Niven and Ondaatje sat next to each other. I recall a friendly boy, with well-groomed hair and quiet good manners. He was better at geography than I was, but not at English. He grew into the grizzled Booker Prize winner of today, still friendly and well-mannered. In his masterly novel *Warlight* he thinly disguises Dulwich College, but he plants giveaways immediately recognizable to anyone who was at the school alongside him.

At Dulwich I was given opportunities that I took for granted and now realise were unique. Perhaps our most famous living alumnus was P. G. Wodehouse; when editing the school magazine, *The Alleynian*, I wrote to him at his home in New York and invited him to write a short contribution. I knew that he had for decades been given a weekly report on how the College had fared in cricket and rugby, so it was not too high a risk to approach him. He replied with two pages of a handwritten letter explaining, wittily and elegantly, why he would never write such a piece and, furthermore, would resist any attempt to get his autograph. He finished with a flourish: 'Yours sincerely, P. G. Wodehouse'. To this day I regret my generosity in giving that letter to my late friend Huw George, a Wodehouse devotee, whence it disappeared into a void.

Tucked away in a ramshackle corner of the school grounds, behind a grill and ignored by everyone except me, was a derelict boat, its white paintwork long mouldered into an indeterminate grey and its provenance unexplained. It was just possible to make out the lettering of its name: *James Caird*. This was the lifeboat in which Ernest Shackleton, an old boy of the college, had with five companions sailed for help from Elephant Island to South Georgia in 1916 when his main vessel, the *Endurance*, was crushed by pack ice and his crew stranded. One of the greatest maritime feats of all time, and still cited over a hundred years later as a master class in team management, the little vessel at the centre of the story lay unloved and virtually unnoticed until a more commercially minded era began to understand its potential in the 1980s and restored it as the show piece it is today.

Looking back I see the neglect of the *James Caird* as part of a pattern of unimaginative self-satisfaction which affected many aspects of the College in my day and which has always made me slightly resistant to its appeals for money, even when I know how much I owe it in so many ways. Nearby was the Dulwich Picture Gallery, founded in the early nineteenth-century around a collection assembled for the last King of Poland. One of the great private art collections in the world, I was never taken to it as part of the school's programme; it was simply never mentioned. I eventually discovered it for myself and would wander in to bask in the glories of Rembrandt, Murillo, Gainsborough and Reynolds, but no thanks to the school which owned it. I later learned that the College possessed the original copy of Philip Henslowe's Diary, which records so much crucial information about how Elizabethan and Jacobean theatrical life was organised. It might have lain in Texas or Melbourne for all that enthusiastic students of English literature like me were allowed near it. Yet the school honours boards, citing examination achievements of the brightest pupils, were regularly updated, and the hall displaying the valour of old boys who had won the Victoria Cross was kept spic and span. Cricketing heroes who had once passed through the College, such as Trevor Bailey, were cited as role models. Dulwich College in my time was a school at which you had to do well. Ideally this would be equally in sport and academia. Being a good actor or debater was second best, but still acceptable. To shine at nothing, except perhaps in decency as a human being, advantaged one not at all.

I left the school at the end of July 1963 with tears rolling down my cheeks. To this day the singing of 'Now Thank We All Our God', with which every school year closed, brings a lump to my throat. When, as vice-captain of the school, I had to sing a sentimental verse of the 'Goodbye Song' at the annual summer miscellany, I again nearly broke down as sentiment overwhelmed me. It was spiced, however, by some resentment. I was embarrassed at nineteen and a half to be still wearing a school cap and asserting tiny meaningless privileges such as being allowed to leave my blue and black striped blazer unbuttoned. I had shown my bolshiness by refusing to attend beatings when, incredible as it sounds nearly sixty years later, the captain of the school summoned his prefects to witness him strapping young boys who had dared to run in the College cloisters or who had been caught smoking a fag behind the bicycle sheds. It was clearly time for me to go and I have very rarely gone back.

*

Growing up in London in the 1950s and early 1960s meant frugality and simplicity. There was still rationing in the early years and choice was a word we hardly understood. I often accompanied my mother when she was out shopping. Indeed, if she spent too long chatting to a neighbour, which she almost always did, I would stand meekly beside her with a seraphic smile whilst I pinched her quietly on the upper part of her arm. If the conversation went on even longer than usual, I would resort to desperate measures – throwing sand into the eyes of an old lady from a few houses away, saying I felt faint to another. We grew up thinking that our mother was not a very good cook. She resorted to scrambled egg, kippers and sausages in a kind of three-day rotation. I realise now that she was scraping along on almost no money and she had little chance to be experimental. I recall those dreadful moments when my father would come home from work, open his clothes cupboard and yell 'Where's my suit?' Mother had pawned it because she was financially desperate. He was probably as bereft of ideas as to how to make do on a lowly police income as she was, dependent entirely on the amount he doled out to her each week as housekeeping money, but it was not conducive to a calm family atmosphere. He was particularly cross in the mornings, and it was rare for me to go to school without having heard him rant about the absence of a towel or the fact that one of us had moved the soap. I needed that half hour walk or cycle ride to steady myself and sometimes to wipe away tears. On one occasion I wrote to his sister's husband, Randolph Whately, senior partner in a well-known solicitors' firm, beseeching him to ask my father to desist from so much shouting. I think he did talk to him and certainly wrote back sympathetically to me, but it made little difference. Father shouted, Mother wept, and Colin and I were sad and sank our energies into school life as best we could.

There was not much glamour in the 1950s, even if it was the era of Marilyn Monroe and Diana Dors. We slunk off to the cinema when we could, which brightened life, but without a car and with so little money we rarely went anywhere. Contact with our large network of Scottish relatives relied mainly on them staying overnight if one of them had business in London. We went once a year for a fortnight's holiday to a seaside resort: Silloth sometimes, or Seaford, Littlehampton or Swanage, but my father did not usually join us. Instead he either went off with the Territorial Army to a camp or with police chums to play golf or to stay with his brother, who had retired from the Indian army after independence in 1948 and become first a shepherd in Scotland and then a factor in Oxfordshire. I loved these special weeks with my mother. As my brothers grew older and more independent it would sometimes just be the two of us walking on the South Downs or straying past the quick sands to the boggy fields at Burgh by Sands, where Edward I had died in 1307 and which marked the most westerly part of Hadrian's Wall.

Twice a year there were moments of sparkle. On New Year's Eve my parents would go to a Scottish party given by our doctor and his wife, Peter and Emily Taylor. Mother would borrow a diamond bracelet from Mrs Gutteridge in the house opposite – 'I think they are real!' she would say. In a long dress that was most likely a cast off from her elder sister in Hucknall, she and my father would sail off into the night, leaving Mrs Gutteridge to pop in every hour or so to see that my brothers and I were alright, and for twenty-four hours a truce would prevail. The other occasion was November 5th each year. Though we occasionally went to services at the Presbyterian Church of Scotland in East Dulwich, my paternal grandmother's strict non-conformism had not been passed on. Guy Fawkes Night was an occasion to light bangers and rockets, gather round a roaring bonfire, and keep the cat in, rather than gloat over Roman Catholic terrorists. I often made the Guy out of old clothes and sacking. Apart from the year that our French exchange student Jacques Lavorel deliberately let the cat out of the house and tied a Chinese cracker to his tail, these were amicable evenings and I loved them, however politically incorrect they seem today.

I was a rather horrid child, but I managed to keep friends. We would spend hours exploring the grassy bomb craters off Denmark Hill, before the blocks of red brick council flats went up. We were advised to be careful. There was, after all, the awful Rebecca-like warning of what had happened to Mary Rand's Dad from up the road. Whilst on holiday in Selsey on the south coast, a place where we ourselves had had a family fortnight not long before, he had taken the dog for a walk on the beach and stepped on a mine. The dog found its way home, but he, alas, did not. Postwar dangers loomed large. They could take, as they do today, the form of predators stopping their cars on the hill and asking if you would like a lollipop. When that happened, I ran screeching home, shouting 'Mummie, Mummie!' at the top of my voice. (We always spelt it Mummie, by the way, a hangover Scoticism.) Our overgrown garden, with its creepy dank Anderson shelter, took years to tame. To my father's credit, he did eventually take it into hand, but not before I had sampled a good display of the fruit of some deadly nightshade and was rushed to hospital to be jumped on until I vomited.

School activities became the centre of our lives. On Saturday afternoons, even before I became a pupil there, I would accompany my mother, and sometimes my father too, to a rugby match at Dulwich College. I shall never forget the dreadful moment when a star of the First Fifteen, Geoffrey Higgs, was laid low by an awkward tackle. We were standing on the touchline with a doctor friend of my parents, Mitchell Thom, when the accident happened. Higgs was prone on the ground until 'Uncle Mitchell', as we called him, came back to where we were standing. 'It's very serious,' was all he said. An ambulance arrived, driving on to the pitch. Six months later, having been made captain of the school in the meantime, the injured lad died.

Occasionally I broke free, when I was old enough to do so, and took myself off to Wimbledon where after 4 p.m. one could get into the Centre Court for the All England Lawn Tennis Championships almost free of charge. There I saw Rod Laver, Ashley Cooper, Christine Truman, Angela Mortimer and, *elegance sans pareil*, Maria Bueno. Occasionally I would wander to the Dulwich Hamlet football ground and watch the most famous of amateur soccer teams, in their distinctive blue and pink colours, feeling slightly traitorous as I did so because we were definitely a rugby family.

As the day approached for me to leave Dulwich College, I decided to write a history of this area where I had grown up. I researched it quite well, discovering the derivation of street names and finding out more about such arcane topics as the Camberwell Beauty, the River Effra and Pickwick Cottage. For the period, which was before foreign travel became mass produced, I suppose I had more than average opportunities to get away: my two week summer holiday on the coast, some trips back to Scotland for weddings and one memorable shooting trip to the firth of Tay with my cousin Donald Niven, visits to family friends who farmed in Devon, two school trips to Italy and one to Greece, and the Rafter Player tours. Cambridge was to be the next step, but only after, just to be different from the rest of the family, I had applied to Oxford. I was interviewed at Lincoln College by the Rector, the celebrated historian V. H. H. Green, upon whose character John Le Carré was said partly to have based George

Smiley. Sadly I made no impression on him. My interview at Gonville and Caius College in Cambridge went better. 'What are you reading at the moment?' I was asked, a standard question that I was later myself to put to countless applicants for university places. '*Rebecca* by Daphne du Maurier,' I replied, too caught on the hop to say anything but the truth, though knowing that *Ulysses* or *On the Road* would have been a better answer. 'What a sophisticated reply!' was the response. I was home and dry. What I only found out later was that my mother had written to the College on each occasion that my brothers and I applied for admission, reminding them that her father had been a Fellow there forty or more years before. My edition of Alexander Mair's poems still has the mutilated pages of Grierson's introduction loose in the book, evidence of how, in the days before photocopying, she had cut them out to send to the College by way of support for her sons' applications. Such is the devotion of mothers.

3

UNIVERSITIES: CAMBRIDGE, GHANA, LEEDS, STIRLING, 1960s and 1970s

Cambridge University was a shock to my system. Partly by dint of being there so long, I had ended up at Dulwich as a biggish fish in a small pond. Suddenly I was no one because everyone else seemed to be someone. My fellow undergraduates were all either highly intelligent or shone at a sport or at acting or in the Union. I now moved from being a capable student of English who won school prizes to being decidedly average intellectually. Our main tutor at Caius College was Donald Davie, a front-ranking poet and notable scholar of eighteenth-century literature. He marked me out in my first term as clearly promising by pairing me for his supervisions with the brightest student of our year in the subject, Gavin Edwards, who went on to have a distinguished career as an academic in Wales. Davie's confidence in me lasted only that term and I was moved to a separate pairing, this time with an amiable Kenyan, Henry Owuor, who was to become a successful business journalist in Nairobi.

I tried to make up for my academic ordinariness by continuing my debating career. The Cambridge Union was in the hands of a Conservative oligarchy, led by a future Chancellor of the Exchequer, Norman Lamont. Despite having run the Public Schools Debating Association and debated with the best school talent of the time, I found myself too nervous and too intimidated to flourish in these self-consciously august and narcissistic surroundings. I was a flop.

My attempts to shine in acting were no less feeble. The big student stars of the day were Germaine Greer and Sally Kinsey-Miles, later as Sally Beauman to be a best-selling novelist and wife of one of the leading classical stage actors of his generation, Alan Howard. I appeared in some good productions, notably at the A.D.C. in John Whiting's *The Devils*, an adaptation of a novel by Aldous Huxley, and in a Caius rediscovery of a forgotten comedy by a former Fellow, Thomas Shadwell, called *A True Widow*, in which I played the disapproving Puritan, Mr Lump. Because of its rarity, the London press came to review this. *The Financial Times* gave me a favourable mention, the second time I had been cited in that prestigious paper. A few months earlier I had attended a recital in the Royal Festival Hall by the soprano Elisabeth Schwarzkopf and an *FT* reviewer scathingly commented on the member of the audience in seat G12 who had not once lowered his opera glasses while the glamorous star was singing.

Capable but not outstanding academically, pedestrian in the debating chamber, thespianly challenged, I had one small triumph. I won a competition organized by Great St. Mary's Church for writing words to a new hymn. My entry may have been the only one they received, but it was set to music and the congregation duly sang it at a Sunday service. My upright grandmother was thrilled and sent me some money. I tried to make a go of it in love. Anne Tan was my first serious girlfriend, a Singaporean of Chinese descent studying English literature at Girton College. Her mother ran an expensive shop in Singapore which specialised in Jensen silverware. She had a younger brother, Ee'Tsing, whom my parents took in during a couple of his school holidays whilst Anne and I were at Cambridge. Anne enjoyed life, briefly joining the Rafter Players for what turned out to be its last tour, playing Maria in a revival of our *Twelfth Night*. We talked literature a lot, speculated on a future together which neither of us really believed in, and went to a lot of parties. We swore undying fidelity and then never saw each other again. A fitful correspondence petered out quite soon.

Cambridge is a beautiful city and I would sporadically take advantage of it by walking to Grantchester or sunning myself on the riverbanks. I had what I still regard as the best undergraduate accommodation in the university, O10, the mock Gothic tower of Caius College which at that time comprised two turret rooms, linked by a spiral staircase. Up this would trudge my 'bedder'. She was an elderly retainer, bringing me each morning my ewer of hot water. The main room had a spectacular outlook down the length of Cambridge's main street, King's Parade. It was there one day I saw a fleet of bathtubs being rowed along by teams of apparently naked young people. The telling aspect of this was that passing pedestrians barely glanced towards it. 'Oh, another fleet of bathtubs with naked undergraduates' was clearly going through all their minds. I had a similar experience when on my 21st birthday I went to pay into my bank account a cheque for £10 sent by my aunt Rosaleen. The problem – or I anticipated it would be a problem – was that she had composed an epic poem celebrating the occasion on the full length of a toilet roll. In those days cheques were only valid if the payer's signature appeared over a 2d stamp. I had to unfurl the whole 'bog roll' before the bored eyes of the clerk at the desk before I could pay it in. He was not so much unamused as keen to show that nothing in Cambridge could ever be original.

I loved my suite of rooms. It was there that a friend brought me news on 22nd November 1963 of President Kennedy's assassination. Only a couple of hours earlier my mother had contacted me to tell me that our beloved family dog, Mickey, a blue roan cocker spaniel of impeccable pedigree, had died unexpectedly of kidney failure. I went round to various friends that evening to tell them about this tragedy and was put out that they were giving priority to the other one of the day. The world could be hard to fathom sometimes.

In my second year I was dispatched to a bedsitter way past Cambridge railway station. There my landlady came in one afternoon to tell me that Winston Churchill had died. I went into London a few days later to walk silently past his coffin as he lay in state in Westminster Hall, pleased to be witnessing real history. In my final year, when I living in the late 1950s architectural miracle that is Harvey Court, my route to dinner at Caius would take me over the Cam and through the grounds of King's College, where I would sometimes encounter E. M. Forster shuffling along into his own evening meal. Just once I bearded him and said what a privilege it was to meet him. 'Do you *truly* think so?' he asked, shy but warm.

I know how fortunate I was to study at Cambridge and be part of a convivial, historic college with a strong reputation in the subject I was reading. I still love the city, to which I have returned many times, but though I look back on my three years there with gratitude I am not sure I do so with much affection. All of us studying English were dismayed when Donald Davie announced towards the end of our first year that he was leaving to become the first professor of English at the new University of Essex. In his place a young don called Jeremy Prynne was promoted to be our Director of Studies. Though he had published a collection of poems, *Force of Circumstance*, which he later made a point of omitting from his canon, we did not then know that he would in time become possibly the central figure in a poetry movement called the English Revival. All we saw was an inexperienced, remarkably pale, effete young man who rose late in the day and offered good dry sherry at supervisions. He always wore a black corduroy jacket, grey flannel trousers, a white shirt and an orange tie. Thirty years later when I went to hear him lecture on the topic 'The Vocative Oh!' he was wearing the same uniform, though I imagine the actual garments had been replaced with replicas in the intervening years. We assumed he was homosexual and were amazed to discover that he had a wife and family and spent his weekends, just as my father so often did, undertaking field exercises with the Territorial Army.

Students at that time were 'farmed out' to other colleges for specialist supervisions. I was fortunate to sit briefly at the feet of the great expert in modern Irish literature, Thom Henn, and to imbibe Helena Shire's brilliant insights into medievalism. I heard commanding lectures on Shakespeare from Anne Righter (later Barton) and Barbara Everett, and on Ibsen from John Northam. Twice the father of English studies at Cambridge, F. R. Leavis, returned to give sweepingly polemical lectures, denouncing and pronouncing in equal measure. 'In a world with so much great literature,' he averred, 'there can be very little time for Trollope and none at all for J. B. Priestley'. One morning I was walking along the pavement in King's Parade when Leavis stepped off the kerb into the path of an oncoming car. I yanked him back and like to think I saved his life. Years later I had an appointment with his daughter Kate who was then working for the Greater London Council and remarked on this. 'Oh, if you could only see him now,' she said sadly. 'We gave him a Christmas present and all he was interested in was the brown wrapping paper'. That mighty intelligence had dimmed, though his legacy survives to this day.

I had little idea of what I wanted to do after Cambridge, but I was sure it should include foreign travel. I had never been outside Europe, but my father's and grandmother's association with Burma greatly influenced me in this determination. One day in the autumn of 1965 I found myself in a corridor at Caius that I did not normally frequent. There on a notice board was an advertisement for Commonwealth Scholarships, to be held in a number of African countries. The closing date for application was the next day. I went back to my room, wrote a letter and posted it, all within a couple of hours of seeing the notice. If I had not been in that unfamiliar corridor that afternoon or in it only twenty-four hours later, my life would have evolved very differently. It was what I have called over the years 'my Thomas Hardy or *Sliding Doors* moment', thinking of a fatal letter slid under a door in *Tess of the D'Urbervilles*, which is not seen because it slipped under a mat, or the apparently inconsequential choice Gwyneth Paltrow makes in the film when her hesitation as whether to board a tube train in London turns out to be life-changing. My whole career and my marriage resulted from that split second when for no good reason I explored a corner of the college I had not been in before.

A few weeks later I was summoned for an interview at Marlborough House, headquarters of the Commonwealth Secretariat. The panel was chaired by a formidable Labour politician, Dame Alice Bacon. I was offered the Scholarship shortly after. The award was always described as being for outstanding young people who were expected to go on to make significant contributions to their country's development, and I was very pleased at the outcome. Only much later did I find out that there had been hardly any British applicants at the time and some delight that a person from the United Kingdom had actually put himself forward to go a developing country, showing that the Commonwealth Scholarship and Fellowship Plan truly worked both ways and was not just about Third World dependency. I think they would have offered the award to the office cat if it had been British. It was confirmed that I would be going to the University of Ghana, where I would study for an M. A. in African literature.

In the long break between graduating in June 1966 and going to West Africa in October, I went on three expeditions abroad. The first, to Scandinavia and Russia, was with the Rafter Players. Then, with my friend Martin Robertson and his brother Andrew, I visited the Faroe Islands, where we camped for three weeks. We had gone there because we had never met anyone who had been and because it was relatively cheap. Gulls swooped and we shielded our eyes to prevent them being plucked out. The puffins clung to steep cliff-sides in their thousands. The wind wailed and the rain lashed down. We came across a beached whale which had died giving birth, stinking but strangely touching in its abandonment. We walked, we climbed, we clambered aboard fishing vessels in the fjords and we occasionally had a good meal of cooked herring in one of Thorshavn's tiny restaurants as an alternative to tinned baked beans inside our damp tent. One day when walking through drizzle on a remote hillside the mist parted and through it emerged the unmistakable bulk of the poet John Betjeman. 'What on earth are you doing here?' we asked by way of introduction. 'Writing an article on Faroese ecclesiastical architecture for *The Daily Telegraph*, dear boys,' came the reply.

My third trip that summer, substantially by rail, was to Venice, then down through Yugoslavia to Greece, and back home via Salzburg, with friends Godfrey Barker and Huw George, with both of whom I had been at Dulwich and Cambridge. We were an unlikely trio, Godfrey and Huw only united though friendship with me rather than with each other. There were tensions most of the time and by the end of the six-week holiday we were clearly destined for different paths in life. I had seen such beautiful places, however, and my appetite for more adventures overseas, this time outside Europe, was ravenous.

*

I arrived in Ghana totally ignorant of the country. My three holidays in the summer had left no time for the homework I know I should have done in advance. I will never forget the warm clamminess of the air thumping my face as I emerged from the Ghana Airways VC10 in Accra, surrounded for the first time in my life only by black people. I lived for the next three years in Commonwealth Hall, one of the elegant residences in this most formally designed of campuses. The University of Ghana lay in Legon, about ten miles outside of Accra. The buildings were vaguely Chinese in inspiration. Within each courtyard were lily ponds, home for the myriad of frogs which croaked throughout the evenings. The university buildings rose from the flat entrance to the campus along a broad avenue to a steep hill, at the start of which stood Commonwealth Hall. The administrative buildings, in which the Vice-Chancellor worked, presided at the top of the hill. Alex Kwapong, the first Ghanaian to head his national university, was an urbane classicist, who later became President of the Association of Commonwealth Universities and later still served with distinction at the United Nations University in Tokyo.

At the time I lived there, the campus was exquisitely maintained. Balme Library was among the best academic collections in Africa, and the nearby botanical gardens a source of endless delight. I was reprimanded on one occasion by a hall porter for airing a shirt on the balcony of my room. Years later, on a return visit, the library had been looted, the ponds were empty of water, and student laundry was drying wherever one looked. But then the university had grown to four times the size it had been in my day and student accommodation was at a premium. Rooms intended for single occupation were now shared by as many as four students. Nothing, however, could blight the boldness of the original concept and to my eye Legon remains among the most beautiful of university sites.

I embarked on my M.A. with astonishing ignorance. 'What did you think of *Things Fall Apart*?' was the first question the head of English Department, a droll Scotsman called Douglas Duncan, asked me on my first day. 'Do you mean the Yeats poem?' I replied. I had never heard of Chinua Achebe or his already epoch-defining first novel, published only eight years before. Achebe had taken his novel's title from Yeats's 'The Second Coming', with which I was familiar, but there was no disguising my lack of preparation for the task ahead. I made up lost ground as speedily as I could by reading just about every work of African fiction and collection of indigenous verse I could find. I soon settled into a routine. For my M.A. thesis I decided to explore critical reactions to West African novels written in English between 1952 and 1968. Before I left Cambridge Jeremy Prynne, in response to my telling him that I was off to Ghana to study African literature, had asked me, more as a statement than a question, 'Is there any?' It was a common enough query at the time, as though a continent five times the size of Europe could be bereft of storytelling, praise poetry or any kind of writing.

In contrast with Cambridge, where studying a living writer was almost inconceivable, almost every novelist, poet and dramatist to whom I now referred was very much alive and publishing. Critical responses to them were changing almost as fast as they wrote. In the 1950s and early 1960s the standard way of praising an African author was to compare him with a western model – he reminded the reader of Dickens or was as inventive as Joyce. Emulating the great writers of another tradition was a desired objective rather than evidence of what in Australia they were already calling 'the cultural cringe': obsequious obeisance to colonial culture. The mindset was, however, slowly changing.

When I arrived at Legon, undergraduate courses in English and history were largely rooted in the canon set by British universities, but they were beginning to adapt, or to decolonize, as it would now be put. I was invited from the start to undertake tutoring and found myself teaching inappropriately esoteric English texts – a novel by Ivy Compton-Burnett, a play by Christopher Fry, some poems by W. H. Auden – to African first year students, many of whom had come from villages and remote communities. The inclusion of a recent novel by Achebe indicated some opening out, so that by the time I left three years later, the courses had been substantially Africanised, with the teaching of novels by James Ngũgĩ, plays by Wole Soyinka and poems by Christopher Okigbo. Responsible literary criticism no longer cited English classics as the standard for all good writing but found their own aesthetic reference points from within Africa itself. History syllabuses moved from being the story of English monarchs and the rise of western capitalism to focusing on African societal organization before the arrival of colonialism and emergence of African nationalism after it. All this amounted to a profound intellectual revolution, achieved without much of a struggle. I was a privileged observer of, and small participant in, these epic transitions.

Although most of my reading and research was done within Legon itself, I also spent short periods at the Universities of Ibadan and Lagos in Nigeria. There could be no question of visiting eastern Nigeria, where many of the best writers I was studying had originated, because in July 1967 the Nigerian civil war broke out following Biafra's secession. Travel to the west and north of Nigeria remained open and so I was also able to visit great centres such as Ilorin, Abeokuta, Kano, Jos and Kaduna, but to my lasting disappointment I never reached Timbuktu. Shops in Ghana in this period of political instability were not well stocked and it was a lifeline on occasion to spend a weekend in Lomé, the capital of nearby Togo, where the Hotel du Golfe served superb French cuisine.

I also travelled further afield, for example spending a few days at Fourah Bay, home of the University of Sierra Leone, where I was the guest of Eldred and Marjorie Jones. Eldred was the author of *Othello's Countrymen*, a seminal study of the depiction of black people in Elizabethan and Jacobean drama. He was also laying the foundation stones of *African Literature Today*, which from 1968 onwards became a hugely influential critical journal. He went on to become Vice-Chancellor of his university, the oldest in sub-Saharan Africa, and was also a key adviser to various Sierra Leonean presidents. As a result of a genetic condition, he had been blind for years. Though he learned braille, his wife Marjorie became his eyes. They were the most inspiring team, whom I would occasionally meet in subsequent years when we coincided on conference panels. Eldred had studied at Oxford in the early 1950s and in September 2001 I was invited to his former college, Corpus Christi, to see a performance of T. S. Eliot's *Murder in the Cathedral*, presented by the same cast that had put it on there exactly fifty years earlier. Becket was played by Douglas Duncan, my first head of department in Ghana, but the point of the occasion was to raise funds for a charity established in Sierra Leone by Eldred Jones.

When I first knew that I was going to live in Ghana, I had been excited by the fact that the man who led the country was Africa's most radical political leader, Kwame Nkrumah. With little knowledge of what he was really like, I was saddened by the *coup d'état* which removed him from office on 24th February 1966, more than seven months before my arrival. Having been too young to remember the Second World War and knowing only what it was like to live in a country where we were told we had never had it so good, I was not prepared for the volatile atmosphere of a new nation moving from one unstable regime to another. One Saturday the campus emptied. I asked where all the students had gone and was told they had moved down to Labadi beach in central Accra to watch the public executions which followed an aborted insurrection on 17th April 1967, aimed to depose General Ankrah, the President. I wrote to my parents describing the atmosphere:

There has been an extraordinary week here with no one doing any work since the attempted *coup* last Monday. The whole place has been buzzing with rumours about how it happened. I know quite a lot of people with brothers and fathers in the army and so have got a general picture. It seems to have just been an attempt to get power by a group of junior officers who were annoyed that they hadn't been promoted recently. But it is incredible that they had so much success. By 9 a.m. they had got all the key places in Accra – they needed only seven men to get the airport, which shows how badly defended it must be. But it was foiled literally by one man, an army captain who got admission to broadcasting house by pretending to be a cleaner, and who whipped out a pistol and shot all the people guarding the recording studio. At 10 a.m. he announced over the radio that the *coup* had been unsuccessful, which wasn't in fact true. The rebels who were guarding the army headquarters, post office, etc., heard this announcement and so threw down their arms, when they needn't have done so. It is pathetic that 120 illiterate soldiers can take over the whole of Accra, but it happened. They were all stationed at a town called Ho, about ninety miles away and no one can understand how they got from Ho to Accra in a convoy without being detected. Anyway, it is obvious that the N. L. C. [National Liberation Council] who are the official government have got rotten security. At Christiansborg Castle, where General Ankrah lives, his soldiers ran out of ammunition! Ankrah himself had to escape by a secret passage which leads to the sea, and then swim two miles to safety. Not bad for a man aged about 60! General Kotoka was less lucky at Flagstaff House and so got killed. He was fantastically popular, and was the brains behind the *coup* which kicked out Nkrumah last year. There were two days public holiday to mourn him, and on Wednesday I went down to town for his State Funeral. I have never seen such a vast crowd anywhere. It was all very jolly with people drumming and wearing their brightest clothes, but this is all part of the set-up here. People from the university were allowed into the Cemetery for the burial and we stood right beside the grave. It was absolutely chaotic with the Bishop fainting half way through, and the police having no control over the crowds at all. But then everyone sang 'Lead Kindly Light' which almost sounds rather good when 300,000 people are singing it. The latest rumour is that Nkrumah is behind the *coup*, but there doesn't seem to be much truth in it. Still, it only needs him to parachute a few troops in one night and it looks as though he could make a come-back easily.

Nkrumah, of course, never returned and died in Romania in 1972 after long exile in Guinea. Years later, in 2010, back in Ghana for a holiday with my family, we visited the mausoleum in which he and his Egyptian wife Fathia now lie, an honour inconceivable to imagine back in the late '60s. We looked around admiringly, taking note of photographs which showed the late President dancing with the Queen, greeting Mao Tse-tung and J. F. Kennedy, addressing crowds and celebrating state events, a handsome man usually dressed in his *kente* toga and wreathed in smiles. There was only one other person present, a lady who came up to us quietly and asked how we had found the place. She was Kwame Nkrumah's only daughter, Samia, a British-educated politician in her own right. She told us that she only visited her parents' tomb once a year and then only for a brief time. That we should coincide with her annual visit and have the opportunity to talk to her at length about her father and his legacy seemed almost to make up for his absence in Ghana when we were living there over forty years earlier.

During his time in power Nkrumah had recruited many specialists from Russia, Eastern Europe and the socialist bloc to assist in the nation's development. One such was Alan Nunn May, who had served over six years in prison for espionage. He came to the University of Ghana in 1961 to work on solid state physics, no British or American university being willing to offer him a post. I asked him on one occasion where one hid stolen classified documents, before passing them on to Soviet Russia. 'That's easy,' he replied. 'You leave them in the most obvious place in your house, in my case face upwards on the telephone table'. He claimed that it was thus that the police, who had raided his home several times, turning up every carpet and floorboard, had missed spotting what they were looking for.

I loved my years in Ghana, which were extended as I was appointed to a lectureship on completion of my M.A. After an initial bout of loneliness, I had an excellent social life. My closest friend was Jean Le Guen, a fellow Commonwealth Scholar, from Mauritius. His subject was chemistry, in which he would vainly try to instruct me to a level beyond what I had achieved at Dulwich. Jean eventually married the next British Commonwealth Scholar to arrive on campus after me, Ruth Banfield, who also researched into contemporary African literature. They came to live in London and had highly successful careers as civil servants, Jean becoming an expert on travel safety. He had the dubious distinction of forecasting dreadful rail crashes at Hatfield in 2000 and at Potters Bar in 2010, his advice having been ignored by governments of the day.

Jean and I sought entertainment in the down-at-heel cinemas of central Accra, seeing old westerns and early Bollywood spectaculars. Only rarely did a new film come. As for theatre, apart from an occasional comedy by the ebullient local dramatist Joe de Graft or a student production of an African play, there was little on offer. I joined an amateur society to play Aguecheek in *Twelfth Night* alongside Paul Danquah, who had been in the film of *A Taste of Honey*, but was now a barrister back in Ghana. The actors James Cairncross, Judi Dench and Barbara Jefford came for recital programmes. As Dench gave her all in the murder scene from *Macbeth*, the audience around me giggled. I pompously asked what was funny. 'What man listens to his wife like that?' came the reply. I have met Dame Judi since and she still remembers this, though sadly she does not so readily recall that we danced together at a British Council party the next day. Those giggles were nothing to the risible response to Laurence Olivier's blacked up performance as Othello in the film version of a National Theatre production, which I had seen on stage in England. I revered Olivier's magnetic transposition into full *négritude* until I saw it ridiculed by a black audience.

I made friends with many Ghanaians and was often invited to their rural home. One, James Kofi Agovi, a good-looking man of huge charm and energy who specialised in literature, joined us in Scotland a few years later but sadly died young. Among the students I taught was the elegant Joyce Aryee, who went on to become a prominent politician, holding several ministries in the government of Jerry Rawlings.

Especially memorable was Chris Asher, chief of a community in the Eastern Region of Ghana called Osorase. We stayed at his 'palace' quite often, sitting in on his deliberations with elders of the village as he sorted out boundary disputes and inheritance wrangles. Every meeting would begin with the slaughter of a sheep and pouring of a libation of gin. Chris was hugely charismatic, with the broadest of smiles and the charm of the devil, to which his pronounced stutter only seemed to add. When in my third year in Ghana I was allocated a flat, his niece, Ama, came to live with me as my housekeeper, in exchange for English lessons. She taught me the rudiments of cooking, usually mixing meat with fish or snails. Chris claimed to have fathered 25 children by many women, each of whose names, like his, began with a C. There were Carlton and Constance, Caroline and Chester, Christie and Cordelia and so on. I noticed, however, that he never boasted of his propagation of the species in the presence of his then wife Alice. Years later Chris appealed for my help. He had become a barrister and entered politics. One day a couple of stooges arrived at his home late at night, telling him they had come to kill him. He asked how much they were being paid to do it and, when told the amount, replied by capping it if they would instead murder the person who had sent them. This they agree do to do and duly did. Chris was arrested, tried for murder and sent to prison. He eventually escaped, with Alice's help, disguised as a woman. He made his way through West Africa to Liberia and from there, with the aid of Amnesty International, arrived in London, where he renewed contact with me. All went well with our revived friendship until he asked me if I would sign a photograph of a woman I had never set eyes on, testifying that I had known her for at least three years. He was hoping to bring her to the U.K. I declined the invitation and sadly he never spoke to me again.

The English department was the centre of my life. In my second year Douglas Duncan moved on, replaced as professor by a kindly Welshman, Bryn Davies, who had an eccentric but hospitable wife Bel. There was a good team of teachers in the department, among them a dignified Ghanaian scholar Kojo Senanu, who supervised my M.A.; a fiery Nigerian, Ime Ikkideh; and, on occasion, a young man called George Awoonor-Williams, who as Kofi Awoonor would become one of Ghana's most celebrated novelists before he was killed in the terrorist outrage in a Nairobi shopping mall in 2013. Grandee of the department was Robin Mayhead, a gay man who had spent most of his career overseas, though he was steeped in the Leavisite mode of critical discourse. He designed a special course for me to take on Henry James because he felt I would need a break from African writing. Making my way through James's *oeuvre* over two years was one of the most valuable parts of my experience of Africa! Over cups of tea in his flat, Robin would discuss with extraordinary erudition whatever novel or essay I had been reading, flirting with his houseboy as he did so.

My attention was focused elsewhere. A young woman called Helen Trow had arrived at the university a few weeks before me. A graduate of Durham University, she had originally been posted as a V.S.O. (Voluntary Service Overseas) to the remote coastal village of Denu. Unfortunately, whoever had been intended to come to Legon had not graduated from her home university in Britain with a degree acceptable to Ghana, so at the last moment Helen was switched to fill the university slot. It was not the kind of position which had attracted her to voluntary service and she was hugely disappointed. Eventually, as she developed her teaching skills, her apartment in Mensah Sarbah Hall on the campus became almost like a hostel for V.S.O.s who needed to take a break from their remote areas by spending a few days in the capital city. She acquired a Honda motor bike as a way of getting around and it was that which first attracted me to her. I never had my own transport while living in Ghana and would rely on the tro-tro system of wooden framed lorries which plied the road between Legon and Accra. Helen and Jean Le Guen both had Hondas, which helps to explains why I saw more of them than anyone else.

'The young couple', as we quickly became known, prowled round each other for many months, avoiding any suggestion that we might become an item. When I arrived in Ghana I had a fancy notion that British people maintained standards by wearing white leather shoes. Helen was appalled by this. Since all the male V.S.O.s wore jeans or shorts with canvas trainers, she simply found me embarrassing. I had miscalculated, but at least I was trying to dress appropriately rather than flinging on whatever grubby clothes were to hand. The students were always immaculately turned out, the men in crisp white shirts and grey flannel trousers, the women in colourful local wrappers. I never understood why visiting Europeans had to be so sloppy.

In the Christmas break of our second year Helen and I went on a hitch-hiking trip together to northern Ghana and across the border to Upper Volta, now Burkina Faso. We headed for the capital city, Ouagadougou, memorably eating on arrival one of the best dinners we have ever had in a restaurant called *Le pavillon vert*. The steak and salad had been flown in from Paris that day, in what was listed as just about the poorest country in the world. Our consciences were stirred, but regrettably only a little. We moved on to Bobo-Dioulasso, the country's second city, and one day sharing the back of a Coca Cola lorry we realised we were in love. At the end of that academic year Helen returned to England and accepted a post with the Committee of Vice-Chancellors and Principals. We flew back together, though I knew I would be returning to Ghana at the end of a summer break because I was too deeply into the arrangements for my appointment as a tenured lecturer to withdraw.

En route we stopped off in Tunis, where my next door neighbour from Denmark Hill days, Sarah Davison, was working as personal secretary to the British ambassador. Sarah arranged that we would go on a leisurely driving holiday through Tunisia and Algeria. She invited an American friend to join us. Two things went wrong. First, the American attempted to seduce me. He was not at all attractive and I did not appreciate his interest. Secondly, I fell ill. The two situations were not connected, but it became clear in the fine city of Oran that I was not well enough to continue the journey. We returned to Tunis, where the embassy doctor misdiagnosed my problem as bronchitis. I had had annual bouts of bronchitis as a child and knew that it did not lead to hallucinations and daft ramblings. Fortunately, Helen was sufficiently alarmed to contact my eldest brother Peter, who by now had qualified as a doctor and was based at St. Bartholomew's Hospital in London. He advised immediate return. On arrival at Heathrow he took one look at me, and from the expression on his face, we recognised that I was seriously ill. I was taken to 'Bart's', the first time I had ever stayed in hospital, where I was found to be suffering from cerebral malaria – 'the lethal sort', as my examining doctors tactfully reminded me. The hospital did not specialise in such illnesses so I became the object of much curiosity, especially among young medical students. I was packed with prophylactics and without their intervention would have died. I recall lying in bed thinking that if this was death, then I am calm about it. I have wondered ever since whether nature has a button that it presses when the time comes to help reassure dying people. Later that summer, before returning to Ghana, I was invited to spend a week in the Hospital for Tropical Diseases in London, where I was required to have further tests. It was like a luxury hotel. I could come and go as I pleased, usually attending a theatre *matinée* before returning to a splendid three-course meal which I had ordered earlier in the day off an *à la carte* menu.

I duly took up my new post as a lecturer at Legon, my first paid appointment. I look back on my three years in Ghana as far more educative than the preceding period spent in Cambridge. For the first time I saw my own country with a truly critical eye. Absence may make the heart grow fonder, but it also sharpens one's intellect. I learned how to teach, I embarked on a lifelong crusade on behalf of post-colonial literatures, and I fell in love not only with my future wife, but with a whole nation. Chris Asher had enstooled me as an Asafohene, a warrior sub-chief sworn to come to the aid of Osorase if ever it was threatened. The ceremony involved being carried shoulder high whilst Johnson's baby powder was thrown all over me. I have never been summoned to defend my adopted community and, given the breach in my friendship with Chris, I do not expect to be. Part of my heart remains in Ghana, however. I have occasionally returned. My liking of the people, my admiration for their ancient cultures, and my enjoyment of Ghanaian cuisine never dim.

*

As the most junior person in my department it fell to me to look after the external examiner when he came out annually to vet scripts of the final year students. In 1968 this was A. Norman Jeffares, professor of English at the University of Leeds. He had an astonishing ability to speed read. We would go to the beach with a pile of examination papers, which he would scour in hardly any time and then chatter about the academic world in which he was rather a big player. He was known internationally as perhaps the leading Yeats scholar of his day; he was also a father figure of what was then termed 'Commonwealth literature', precursor of post-colonial discourse. Derry, as he was universally known, was larger than life, a big man physically, with the heartiest chuckle I have ever known and an indestructibly cheerful disposition. I was in awe of him at first, then came to love him dearly, though I was always aware that he had his critics who thought he was too materialistic, entrepreneurial and egotistical. He had a worldwide network and was known as Professor Fixit because he had placed so many academics in their lectureships or chairs. He took a shine to me. One afternoon, sprawled on the sand, surrounded by a scattering of exam scripts and licking an ice cream, he asked me what I planned to do when I left Ghana. 'No idea' was my reply, because, had it not been for Helen returning to London, I was enamoured of the possibility of staying at Legon forever. 'You must do a Ph. D. whilst making up your mind,' he said. What Derry planned always happened, so it was that I found myself registered as an external candidate for a doctorate at Leeds.

Having decided to get married, Helen and I were separated for nine months until I had fulfilled the first year of my contract as lecturer in Ghana. Then, organised by the resourceful Derry, I returned to England and was appointed by him to a temporary lectureship at Leeds. I recall the wonderment with which I opened a letter from him days before I took up the post. He had found a pot of cash which would allow him to raise my salary from £1,200 per year to £1,400! That extra £200 was a lot of money at the time and one of the most appreciated votes of confidence I have ever received. Derry himself was supervising my thesis, which was to be a comparative study of African, Asian and Caribbean fiction in English, focusing on the relationship of the individual to the community. This was a new area of study and no critical theory had yet accreted round it. As supervisor, Derry was conscientious, enforcing deadlines and always returning specimen chapters promptly, with helpful annotation. He was less evident as head of department. The graffiti that appeared on the wall of the School of English one day – 'Derry Jeffares is a figment of the imagination' – summed up what a lot of colleagues felt about his absences abroad and multiple editing and publishing commitments outside of the university.

In the year that I worked in the School, teaching arrangements were in the hands of Geoffrey Hill. He was already a poet of note, *King Log* the previous year having pitched him into the front rank. Later knighted and elected Professor of Poetry at Oxford, Hill came to be regarded by many as the major English poet of his generation. What I saw of him was a kindly man, who understood my nerves at joining one of the best English departments in the world with very little experience. Derry had become convinced that many in his department were resting on their laurels. In his usual swashbuckling way, he asked Geoffrey to sort it out. 'If they've been teaching Victorian poetry for twenty years, give them the eighteenth century. If they think they are Shakespearians, make them Romantics.' Many colleagues reacted to this with irritation, but I was new so I did what I was told and dabbled in various periods according to whatever was allocated to me.

I took part in a couple of plays in the university's Theatre Workshop. My main part was Aubrey, the unsympathetic husband in Pinero's *The Second Mrs Tanqueray*. I came to know Leeds well, though it rarely stopped raining. Whenever I could, I explored the surrounding towns such as Bradford and Wakefield. At first Yorkshire was almost as strange to me as Ghana had been on arrival, though memories came back of a holiday I had enjoyed in Harrogate as a fourteen-year old in the company of a close family friend, Ian Dudgeon. Ian had been invited by his extremely wealthy great uncle and aunt, Wyrral and Gladys Sissons, to stay with them and to bring a companion. I had never been in such a rich home and I delighted in all the curios this childless couple had collected over a long marriage. Unfortunately, my pleasure was spoiled by overhearing Gladys describe me to Wyrral as 'without doubt the clumsiest boy I have ever known'. I do not recall what provoked this calumny, but it is one of those remarks which, once heard, never departs. Now whenever I drop anything or spill my food onto my clothes, which my *über*-observant family tells me happens frequently, I always think back to that comment in Harrogate over sixty years ago.

Much of my time in Leeds was spent getting out of it, not because I disliked it but because of my engagement to Helen. I had been introduced to her parents the previous summer and she to mine. She first met my mother around my bed at St. Bartholomew's Hospital, visiting me in all her finery after having accompanied her parents to a garden party at Buckingham Palace. If one wants to impress one's future in-laws, this is not a bad beginning. Now, a year later, we made plans for our marriage. I spent many weekends staying with Helen's family in Chelmsford. Her father, Claude Trow, was Pro Vice-Chancellor of the City University, responsible among many things for their ambitious programme of building new student residences. He had been a schoolmaster and later was responsible for further education in the County of Essex. Helen's mother, Ella, had died five days after giving birth in May 1945, the result of pre-eclampsia. Such a disaster, my obstetrician brother Peter told me, would be most unlikely to happen now as medicine had moved on.

Claude, based at the time in Monmouth, and left with a baby daughter, had moved to Felsted School near Dunmow. There his colleague, Michael Craze, and his wife Carol, looked after Helen for her first two years. Michael was her godfather and to the end of his life they adored each other. Claude re-married when Helen was two years old, his second wife Jane having been matron at Monmouth Girls' School in the early years of the war, as well as a friend of Ella's. They had a son, Bryan, Helen's half-brother.

Claude took charge of our wedding arrangements. He was a churchwarden at Chelmsford Cathedral so there was no doubt as to where the ceremony would take place. When he learned that I had six surviving uncles and six aunts, most of whom had spouses, 35 first cousins, two brothers and three nephews, most of whom would expect to be invited but few of whom would actually come, he was profoundly gloomy. He did not understand that if a relative of mine, and there were several of them, had sworn never to cross the Scottish border with England, they meant it.

Come the day of our marriage, 22nd August 1970, there were about even numbers on either side of the aisle. The provost, Hilary Connop Price, had given us sympathetic instruction beforehand and all went well. Our reception was held in Shire Hall next to the cathedral and as we walked there, Helen in her long white dress with real flowers in her hair, me holding a huge multi-coloured golfing umbrella, it began to rain. 'Never mind, it means good luck!' said a knowing guest.

That was right, because it has been a lasting and loving marriage. My brother Colin was my best man and made a witty speech, which included a reference to the fact that on the day I was born the favourite for the English Greyhound Derby had, as a result of a taxi door being slammed inopportunely, lost its tail on its way to the race. He hoped the same would not happen to me on my wedding night. It was a good joke, but unfortunately just before he spoke I had whispered to him to avoid anything smutty as Helen's Baptist grandfather was standing nearby. As a result, Colin muttered that part of his speech. Only the bride and groom caught it.

We were whisked away sharply at 5 p.m. English weddings at the time did not last all evening and there were no ceilidhs as there would have been in Scotland. I recall how we looked forlornly through the rear window of our chauffeur driven car as our guests waved goodbye before returning to the party we had left.

We spent our honeymoon in Nerja, southern Spain. We were determined not to draw attention to the fact that we were newlyweds, but the plan came unstuck on the first day. I plunged into the warm sea and dived under water; as I did so, I saw my wedding ring slide off my finger to the sandy bottom. There was nothing for it but, amid tears and panic, to confess to everyone around us on the beach that it had made its first appearance only the day before and its loss was a clear indication of our marital doom. Everyone scoured the area where I'd been swimming, but it was irrevocably gone. Today, whenever I eat fish, I prise it open carefully in the hope that my wedding ring will be inside. After our honeymoon we bought a new one, which the Very Reverend Connop Price kindly blessed anew.

Towards the end of my year at Leeds, I was offered a renewal of my contract for a second year. Helen and I found a house in Headingley, which we looked forward to renting. Then out of the blue came a suggestion from Derry Jeffares that I should apply for a lectureship being advertised at the University of Stirling. It was for a tenured post of the kind I had given up in Ghana. The Leeds appointment was most unlikely to continue into a third year, so I applied. On my way to the interview, the train from Edinburgh to Stirling was seriously delayed. Three times I enquired of the guard what the problem was and when it might arrive. Three times he answered at length in an accent so broad I had no idea what he was saying. I prided myself on being Scottish, yet nothing could have underlined more the contrast between the country to which I was contemplating moving and the one in which I had lived in most of my life. I quickly learned that Edinburgh, which I had stayed in many times since childhood, and almost anywhere due west of it, were demoticly entirely separate areas. Fortunately, my late arrival at Stirling was tolerantly received and I was given the post.

Helen had never been to Scotland. The country had not had a good press in her family. Her parents had been only once, for a holiday in Skye, where it had poured every day and the unforgiving mists had been so thick that they had not seen much beyond the bonnet of their car, let alone a mountain. Once we knew for sure that we would be starting married life in Scotland, we went there for a long weekend to sort out accommodation. We arrived at Stirling station, one of the most impressive in Britain, by overnight sleeper. As we walked into the centre of the town, we coincided with a passing Orange parade. It was the annual 12th July celebration of King Billy's victory at the Battle of the Boyne. I had no idea that this was as big an event to certain west of Scotland Protestants as it was in the north of Ireland. We stood dourly waiting for the procession of bowler hats, banners and drums to pass. It showed no sign of doing so quickly, so we took our chance and tried to dart across the road when a gap appeared. We learned an immediate lesson. On no account does one break an Orange parade. Yanked back, we were told to stay put. This time, even though the accent telling us this was as thick as on the railway train a few weeks before, there was no doubt what was said. It was Helen's introduction to Scotland and mine to Stirling.

Despite this rough start, I was delighted at the prospect of working in Scotland. The nation was renewing itself. Though we were still some way off the referenda of 1979 and 1997 or re-establishment of a Scottish Parliament in 1999, there was no mistaking the intensity of national feeling or that the tide was moving in the direction of greater devolution. For Helen this sometimes presented a problem. She had decided not to use her maiden name but to be known as Niven, a Scottish derivation of the Gaelic *naoimhin*, which means 'little saint'. This gave her some, but not total, protection against transparently anti-English sentiments she frequently ran into: 'Why do you live in Scotland when you are obviously English?' This parochialism was the downside of Scottish aspirations at the time, but there was no doubting that Scotland was on the move, politically, culturally and educationally.

The founding of Stirling University in 1967 was part of this renaissance. It resulted from the Robbins Report of 1963, which had argued that university places 'should be available to all who were qualified for them by ability and attainment' (9). The Report had also advocated the founding of a new university in Scotland, the first that was wholly new since the nineteenth century. Lord Robbins himself became the first Chancellor of Stirling and its young Principal was Tom Cottrell, a distinguished chemist who gathered round him an innovative team determined not just to copy the practices of every other Scottish university.

The department I joined in September 1970 had turned its face on much academic tradition. We had no conventional examinations; degree results were built around a system of periodic assessment whereby students submitted the best examples of their work. I was thrilled by this, having nursed the feeling that I myself would have had a better degree if I had been able to be judged by the high marks I usually scored for my undergraduate essays rather than what I was able to recall in a nervy three-hour session being stared at by suspicious invigilators. When it began, the department of

English Studies comprised only lecturers who had experience of working outside Britain as well as within; there was thus a natural sympathy with the specialism I had been appointed to oversee, Commonwealth literature. The head of department, Tommy Dunn, had published very little but had held a chair at the University of Lagos in Nigeria, where he had tested the idea of abandoning the traditional chronological exposition of English literature – the *Beowulf* to Virginia Woolf approach – in favour of introducing students to the subject through modern authors. In their first year at Stirling no one reading English would encounter Shakespeare or Dickens until they had eased themselves into the concept of critical discourse through language they could understand and ideas with which they could identify. I recall one of the university's most famous graduates, the novelist Iain Banks, receiving the unheard-of mark of A+ for an essay on the Caribbean writer Wilson Harris. I asked him how he could be so brilliant in one area of literature and so ordinary in others. 'Easy,' he replied. 'When I write on Harris there is no body of opinion telling me what to say. If I wrote an essay on *Hamlet* or Jane Austen telling you I think they are crap, you would mark me down'. 'No I wouldn't,' I remonstrated unconvincingly, 'not if you said why.' But we both knew he was right. Under the Stirling system students were encouraged, by the nature of what they studied and when it was approached, to be themselves and to be sceptical of received judgements.

We operated a semester system, two a year as opposed to three terms. Stirling at the time was unique in the country in doing this. It led to a longer Christmas break and an earlier return to the campus in autumn than any other university. There could be problems with this. It meant, for example, that the drug purveyors, pursuing first-year students who had not lived independently before, plied their evil trade at Stirling ahead of anywhere else. Generally, however, we were proud of our individualism and the university in its early years flourished, as it does again now. On 12th October 1972, however, an event occurred which, though intended to celebrate the university's success, nearly led to its demise. The Queen visited the campus. There were plenty of warnings that trouble might lie ahead. For a start there was the international context: since riots at the Sorbonne in France in 1968 there had been waves of demonstrations in universities around the world; there was no reason to suppose that Scotland, in the political mood it was in at the time and with its west coast republicanism, would be exempted. Stirling also had its particular grievances. A greenbelt site, it was still building its core facilities. It was these the Queen was coming to inspect and declare open, but many students felt that their own needs had not been priorities in the construction programme.

I attended a staff meeting a few days before the visit. The university secretary was Sir Derek Lang, who had previously been Governor of Edinburgh Castle and in effect head of the Army in Scotland. Young, articulate, well-informed members of the academic community rose one by one to speak of the student unrest which was evident on campus and to ask what contingency plans were in place if things should go wrong. Sir Derek blandly batted away every objection with references to the fact that he had received Her Majesty on many military occasions in Edinburgh and there was no need to be concerned.

Come the day I was in the central hub of the university, named from that day Queen's Court, when the Queen, prettily dressed in pink, arrived. Many well behaved students were delighted to greet her, but others had been drinking from an early hour, the powers that be having ignored advice to close the campus shop that morning. I stood next to an American student who I knew had arrived at the university only a few days before. 'Fuck off, you Hun!' she yelled in the Queen's ear as she passed by. Later Her Majesty was invited to cross what is known as the link bridge, which traverses Airthrey Loch at the centre of this most rural and picturesque of university settings. The bridge was lined with students, some of whom jeered. A photograph of one of them, quaffing from a wine bottle, was to go round the world later that day.

That evening I met Helen, who by now was working for the Open University in Edinburgh, off her commuter train at Dunblane station. She asked how the day had gone. 'It couldn't have gone worse!' I replied. She did not really believe me until a little while later we watched the television news, on which the story of the

Queen's visit to Stirling University was the top item. Nor was that the end of the story. The episode caused huge harm to the university's reputation. Applications fell so dramatically that there was talk of closing it down. Many students signed a letter of apology, which was sent to Buckingham Palace, but the damage was done. The Queen herself went on later that day to a reception at Stirling Castle, where she was heard to say that Sir Derek had been of no use at all. He resigned a few months later. As for the Principal, I suspect that his heart was broken. He collapsed and died the following June a few days before his 50th birthday and on the very day he was due to explain to the governing body of the university how the visit had turned out as it did. It was a year of tragedy. Two executive members of the student council were killed when driving overnight to the annual conference of the National Union of Students in Kent. The university community was bitterly divided and the happy atmosphere we had encountered on arrival two years earlier was totally dissipated.

In common with several other members of staff I volunteered to help in the re-grouping of the university that had to follow. I became one of the two resident wardens of Murray Hall, one of the larger student accommodation facilities newly built on the campus. We had been living in Dunblane five miles from the university, but now we were on duty 24 hours a day. Though she was fully committed to the Open University, eventually becoming its Scottish Secretary, Helen was inevitably drawn into the student environment.

We would get knocks on the door of our flat at 4 a.m. 'Could I have change for the telephone, please?' 'Have you a railway timetable?' 'I think X is having a miscarriage'. Two students, high on drugs, thought they could fly out of a sixth-floor window; fortunately both survived, but as one had encouraged the other, a prosecution followed in which the only charge that could be brought, according to Scottish law, was Attempted Murder. After two and a half years, we decided to reclaim our lives and so moved back to Dunblane where we had bought a charming terraced house (two houses originally) called Tillymet, in Ramoyle, the oldest part of this ancient town.

Living opposite us was Stewart Sutherland, later to become Lord Sutherland of Houndwood and through his many roles a distinguished contributor to higher education, as well as an outstanding philosopher. Stewart taught me how to hang game because his house had the facility for this. He was only one of many lifelong friends we made whilst at Stirling University. Even in its grimmest moments, it was an extraordinarily hospitable place. We had one ready-made contact when we arrived, Robin Mayhead, who had preceded us there from his post in Ghana. He already had a justified reputation as a literary critic and was general editor of series on major British authors, published by Cambridge University Press, to which he asked me to contribute a volume on D. H. Lawrence. This became my first book, *D. H. Lawrence: The Novels.* (10)

Most of the people who became our friends were still to establish the significant reputations they later attained. Grahame Smith, for example, had newly arrived from Swansea with his wife Angela and a young family, to which was soon added a third child, Dan, who became my godson, just as Angela was later to be godmother to our daughter. Grahame went on to be one of the outstanding Dickensians in the world, as well as an expert on the relationship between film and fiction. His wife eventually took over from me, when I left Stirling, as the specialist in the department on postcolonial literature, as well as an expert on the writings of Katherine Mansfield and Virginia Woolf.

Then there was Michael Alexander, already renowned for his Penguin translation of *Beowulf* and the Earliest English Poems. I introduced him to my doctoral student, Eileen McCall, who was working on West African authors. She was a woman of independent spirit and great beauty. The next thing I knew they were married and before long the parents of two daughters and a son. To everyone's grief, Eileen died of cancer at the age of thirty-seven, a loss to which I am still unreconciled all these years later. However, to our relieved delight, Michael re-married a year afterwards. His second wife, Mary Sheahan, who was Australia's Consul for Scotland, became a devoted mother to the three children, who were all under the age of eight.

Eileen was the daughter of Pat McCall, one of Stirling University's many mature students. These were men and women of experience and usually brilliance who had somehow missed out on taking a degree earlier on. The Open University, Helen's employer, had come into being in 1969 and clearly offered one route for such people, but Stirling, radical from the start, offered another. Pat was one who had taken it up, the historian Monica Clough another.

Our friendships multiplied in this most sociable environment. Felicity Riddy, a medievalist, and her husband John, whose party trick was to fall asleep at their own superb dinners; Alasdair Macrae, an outstanding teacher, and his shrewd kind wife Elise; John McCracken, who wrote the definitive history of Christianity in Malawi, and his wife Juliet, Monica Clough's daughter and a distinguished travel journalist. I joined the department, and also left it, on the same days as Norman MacCaig, who held a post at Stirling in creative writing. Widely regarded as one of Scotland's great poets, he had over forty years before been a student of Alexander Mair at Edinburgh and so was one of only three people I have ever met able to give me a first-hand account of what my grandfather was like as a teacher and scholar. In 1974 Derry Jeffares himself moved to the university from Leeds, bringing his network and academic fame with him as he settled in the delightfully named Fife community of Rumbling Bridge.

I was encouraged, as part of my responsibility to build up the university's reputation in Commonwealth literature, to invite writers to give lectures and go myself to international conferences. Authors visiting Stirling often stayed with us. Shiva Naipaul, who was to die too young, arrived for a night and stayed a week. Thomas Kenneally was more tactful, regaling us with endless tales until the small hours. Samuel Selvon, the humorous chronicler of Caribbean immigrants in London, delighted and appalled us by eating a huge supper the moment his talk was over and then asking for a chicken takeaway as we drove him to Stirling station to catch the overnight sleeper back to London. He was decidedly 'fou' by the time we delivered him to his second-class shared *couchette*, joining a traveller who had boarded in Perth and was now primly tucked up. Smelling of chips and beer, Sam bid us goodnight. We left the citizen of Perth to his nocturnal fate.

Nirad Chaudhuri, author of one of the greatest memoirs ever written, *Autobiography of an Unknown Indian*, although approaching eighty, also took the overnight train to give a talk at the university and later to receive an honorary degree. For the next twenty-three years we remained closely in touch with him and his reticent but shrewd wife Amiya, often visiting them at their home in Oxford. I know of no other author whose idea of delighting a five-year old child was to read to him La Rochefoucauld's Moral Maxims, but it worked for our son every time, especially when accompanied by Chaudhuri removing his false teeth and wiggling his mouth and jaw into extraordinary shapes.

When the university similarly bestowed an honorary degree on Chinua Achebe, he and his wife Christie came to dinner with us. Professor Dunn's wife, Joyce, drawing on her memories of life in West Africa and sounding more patronising than perhaps she intended, asked the celebrated author 'How was the rainy season this year?' He mused with a puzzled expression on his face before politely replying, 'Rather wet I believe'.

In the years that followed, a quiet friendship ensued between us and the Achebes. In 1990 I went to Nigeria to participate in 'Eagle on Iroko', a symposium to mark Chinua's 60th birthday. I was down to speak for an hour immediately after the state governor had opened the event. His Excellency was late arriving: two days late. As this had some impact on the symposium schedule, my chairman whispered to me as I rose to speak, 'You have five minutes, that's all!' Compressing a written lecture planned to last sixty minutes into five is a challenge, which I did not entirely meet, going on for at least twice my newly allotted time. I kept thinking of the British Council, which had paid for me to come all the way from London just for these few moments.

On the day I left I took a photograph of Chinua at his front door. Resplendent in a pink lace *agbada* he strikes a handsome figure. Only a month later he was in an appalling road accident that left him paralysed for life from the waist down. Christie and he moved eventually to Bard College and later Brown University in the United States because of the medical facilities. I visited him in both places, for his 70th birthday and later for a conference. In London I interviewed him onstage in an emotional encounter at the Hackney Empire. Billed as 'Two Nobel Laureates and a Legend', he appeared with Wole Soyinka and Derek Walcott. By the time we met in the evening Chinua, just off a flight from New York that morning, had been in four hotels, the organisers of the event having not taken his disability seriously.

In 2007 Chinua was awarded the Man International Booker Prize. He was not well enough to come to England to receive it, but he and Christie came the following year. Helen and I were invited to a luncheon held in their honour in the House of Lords, hosted by Lord Baker of Dorking. As the guests were departing after a good meal and a few speeches, it occurred to me that the Achebes had had no chance to see the interior of the Palace of Westminster, except for the modest Attlee Room where we had eaten and into which he had been pushed in his wheelchair from an outer courtyard. I asked Kenneth Baker if there was any chance of a tour. Under his tutelage we set off, just the five of us. Parliament was not sitting, and to my amazement we could go anywhere, including the chambers of both Houses. I was not permitted to take a photograph, but the image of this great African writer, scourge of colonialism *par excellence*, surveying from a wheelchair an empty House of Commons, epicentre of the Mother of All Parliaments, imprinted itself on my memory forever.

Chinua died in 2013. His funeral in Ogidi, eastern Nigeria, on 23rd May was attended by over 4,000 people. I was among them, guest of the family. The Presidents of Nigeria and Ghana were there, as well as a personal representative of the Archbishop of Canterbury. To its shame, the British government was the only major government not represented. I sat behind an empty chair marked 'United Kingdom'. I wrote to William Hague, Foreign Secretary at the time, for an explanation of this absence. A reply eventually came from a minion: the British government had not been invited. I knew that to be untrue. I went back to the Achebes' house that evening. There were just a dozen of us, comforting Christie and quietly viewing Chinua's place of internment alongside the house, now that the crowds had dispersed. I am sometimes asked who, among the writers I have met, I most hold dear. Chinua Achebe, I always reply: 'Not just writer, human being'.

I have followed this Achebe thread of nearly forty years, but I now return to 1975. In that year I ran at Stirling the first conference for which I had overall responsibility. It was called 'The Commonwealth Writer Overseas', examining themes of exile and expatriation. Some of the great names of the period came: Chaudhuri was one, but they also included Fleur Adcock, Nuruddin Farah, Wilson Harris, Kamala Markandaya, David Rubadiri, and Randolph Stow. I persuaded Hugh MacDiarmid, to many minds the most important Scottish poet since Robert Burns, to come and read some of his poems. He was in his mid-eighties and frail. His wife accompanied him and Norman MacCaig acted as a kind of chaperone. I was warned that I must not let MacDiarmid drink any alcohol, but on arrival in our flat after the reading he immediately asked for whisky. I relented with the smallest dram I had ever poured. In a stronger voice than he had displayed all evening, he asked as he peered at the drink, 'What's this? There's a dirty wee stain on the bottom of your glass.'

*

My first overseas conference came during my time at Stirling. It was at the University of the West Indies. I travelled there in the company of Anna Rutherford and Hena Maes-Jelinek, already well known as queens of post-colonial literary criticism. Seeking the cheapest way to travel, we boarded a 'plane together in Luxembourg and flew to Nassau in the Bahamas with the intention of picking up a connecting flight to Kingston, Jamaica. On arrival in Nassau we were given free accommodation at the most luxurious hotel I had ever stayed in, the Emerald Beach, and told that our onward B.O.A.C. flight was stranded in London because of freezing fog. We stayed in emerald luxury for two days, during which we mostly sprawled on a private beach, only to find when we eventually arrived at the Mona campus of the university that we had missed the main excitement of the conference. Offended by a questioner, V. S. Naipaul had walked out. Love him or, as many critics did, hate him, the elder Naipaul was recognised by everyone as the outstanding Caribbean novelist and essayist of the day. It would be years hence before I had my chance to meet him. I did, however, encounter for the first time the south Indian writer Raja Rao, about whom I would later write a book. In my diary I wrote, 'Rao is gentle but scrupulous, fascinatingly informative about his own work. He justified the conference for me and, in his art and his humility, was an effective antidote to the generally strident note of this conference'.

I became a member of the Association for Commonwealth Literature and Language Studies (ACLALS), which organised many such academic gatherings. For years I never missed one of them. In Kampala, Uganda, in 1974 I was subjected to a diatribe by a local author called Grant Kimenju, who had been asked to introduce me, which he did for the best part of half an hour. My crime was that I was British. I thanked him politely for his generous welcome and proceeded to give my paper. In 1977 Helen and I visited India for the first time, the Association having been invited to hold its triennial meeting in Delhi. We had both been invited to give lectures after the conference, Helen now being well established at the Open University in Edinburgh and so regarded as an authority on distance education. We were in India for six weeks, travelling across the country to Patna in one direction, Chandigarh, Patiala and Simla in another, and Madras, Mysore and Madurai in a third. It was the first of at least eighteen visits to this most diverse and enthralling of countries.

It was now that I first met Mulk Raj Anand, widely regarded as the founding father of Indian literature in English. I had written a substantial part of my doctorate on his work, having been drawn by the sheer extent of it on the departmental bookshelves in Leeds. Encountering this prolific, often rough-hewn but immensely humane author was a revelation. In the mid-

1930s, Anand's first novel, *Untouchable,* had been hawked around nineteen publishers before, on the recommendation of E. M. Forster, it found a home. Novels and short stories flowed from his pen thereafter, as well as essays, plays, books of art criticism and endless letters, many of which I was to receive in the ensuing years before his death in 2004. I had no doubt that he courted western admiration and was grateful to me for the critical book I had written about his work, *The Yoke of Pity* (11) , but I also knew that he had in his younger days corresponded with some of the great authors of the century, such as André Malraux and Pablo Neruda. Virginia and Leonard Woolf befriended him at the Hogarth Press when he was a student in London, T. S. Eliot took him to lunch, D. H. Lawrence greeted him in Vence three weeks before he died, George Orwell worked alongside him at the BBC during the war, and he had rubbed shoulders with the great socialist politicians of the west, the Soviet Union and China. In India the current Prime Minister, Indira Gandhi, called him 'Uncle Mulk' and his books could be found in every pavement store. He had huge, slightly mischievous charm, his words tumbling over each other as, with endless engagement, he commented upon the world around him. To the end of his life he emanated old-fashioned courtesy, to women especially, which I had no doubt was rooted in the sexual energy of his youth.

In later years I stayed with Mulk several times at his home in Cuffe Parade, Bombay/Mumbai. A rambling romanesque-gothic-baroque-victorian folly of a house, it had been built for a merchant in the mid nineteenth-century. Mulk and his delicate wife Shirin Vajifdar, a former Parsi dancer, occupied only the ground floor. There I was awoken in the middle of one night by a scrabbling sound. I switched on the light to see rats peering from behind every bookend. Stories flooded back of pirates releasing the ship's rats to eat away the toes of their captors. Though Mulk and Shirin explained the next morning that the creatures came in from the garden during the wet season to take shelter, I never again slept a wink in their city house, much as I loved their daytime hospitality. I was more comfortable at their country retreat at Khandala, in the hills behind Pune, where Mulk lived a frugal life half-way between that of a *guru* and that of a *shishya*.

On his last visit to England in 1996, when he was ninety, Mulk came to stay with us. I drove him to the Buckinghamshire town of Chinnor where he had written part of his masterpiece, *Across the Black Waters*, a tale of bewildered Indian sepoys being used as cannon fodder in the First World War. He thought he remembered the house in which he and his first wife Kathleen had lived. We walked up the garden path of a small terraced dwelling and saw through the window a young mother with baby watching morning television. We knocked tentatively. Mulk explained in his rather clotted and highly accented English his association with the house. Mother and child stared until he was finished and then closed the door. Mulk was happy, just as he was the next day when he renewed contact with his old friend, the Labour politician Michael Foot, who he had not seen for decades. I recorded an interview with him for the BBC, but the producer Judith Bumpus told me afterwards that, though she had politely allowed us to go on conversing for an hour, the material was unusable because listeners would have struggled to make out what Mulk was saying.

Mulk Raj Anand, Nirad Chaudhuri and Raja Rao were three *doyens* of Indian prose. Rao, whose great philosophical novel *The Serpent and the Rope* had been a set text for bewildered first year students at Legon, was the least easy to know. His mantra, 'all is silence', was a puzzling reflection from a wordsmith which made personal engagement difficult. His young American wife ensured, however, that he did not disappear completely into rather mannered transcendence. Writers Workshop, an adventurous small press in Calcutta run by the polymath P. Lal, published my study of *The Serpent and the Rope* in 1987, exquisitely bound by Tulamiah Mohiudeen in red and green handloom sari cloth. (12)

There was a fourth horseman of this literary apocalypse, perhaps better known internationally than any of them. This was R. K. Narayan. Like the first three, he lived an exceptionally long life. I knew the others well but had long presumed I'd missed my chance of meeting the creator of the small town of Malgudi, in which he had set most of his novels and short stories. That changed in 2000 when, on a visit for the British Council to Chennai, I casually asked after him, assuming he still lived in Mysore, upon which Malgudi was based. My colleague corrected me, explaining that he was residing in Chennai itself, not a stone's throw from where we were talking. Within minutes I found myself in Narayan's ground floor apartment, which he shared with his nephew. We sat in an enclosed verandah for over an hour, chatting amiably. Though deaf, Narayan was astonishingly welcoming to someone of whom he had never heard. Forever associated with his champion, Graham Greene, he said of him, 'Rather a naughty boy, I'm afraid!', alluding to Greene's many sexual affairs. The conversation was on that level throughout, probing no intellectual depths but bright with gossip and reminiscence. To my sorrow Narayan died the next year. I went back to India for conferences celebrating his birth centenary, as well as Anand's, Rao's and Ahmed Ali's.

*

In 1975 I was granted sabbatical leave for a few months which permitted me to accept an invitation to join the University of Aarhus in Denmark as a visiting professor. I took Anna Rutherford's place while she taught in Nigeria, inheriting her Commonwealth literature courses. It was a convivial place to work and I made many Danish friends. I learned rudimentary Danish and with Helen travelled not only around Jutland but into Norway north of the Arctic circle. Denmark at the time was going through a period of extreme libertarianism. Every kind of opinion, however anarchist or rebellious, could be freely expressed and there was no constraint on what could be visually depicted. I used to look out of my rented room on one of the main streets of Aarhus, Denmark's second city, and see well muffled middle class matrons standing at the 'bus stop outside a porn shop where a giant photograph of an erect penis was displayed the whole time I was there.

Scotland seemed dour by comparison. The Kirk was still influential; shops did not open on Sundays; Good Friday was a solemn day of mourning, and Christmas was almost an ordinary day in contrast to the celebrations of New Year. When on an infrequent Sunday we went to a service in Dunblane Cathedral we would be certain to hear a sermon promising eternal hellfire from the fiery minister, John R. Gray. I had never been confirmed into any church, but under his tutelage I was admitted as a member of the Presbyterian Church of Scotland shortly before he became its Moderator.

For all its Calvinist underlay, I was delighted to be living in Scotland, a thing I had promised myself since childhood. Our surroundings were beautiful all times of the year. We explored Perthshire and Sutherland, Orkney and Galloway, St. Andrews and Cumbernauld. I was able to see more of my cousinage than ever before. We coincided with a rich period for the arts in Scotland, led by the MacRobert Centre at Stirling University itself, brilliantly run by one of the most erudite arts managers in Britain, Anthony Phillips. We almost took it for granted that after a day's work we would have Scottish Opera, the Prospect Theatre Company, 7.84, Vladimir Ashkenazy, Ballet Rambert or Cleo Laine and the John Dankworth Quartet filling our evening. I will never forget the Royal Lyceum Theatre Company from Edinburgh presenting Eugene O'Neill's *The Iceman Cometh* with the great Irish actor J. G. Devlin, or John Kani and Winston Ntshona, in this era of *apartheid*, hushing an audience with a play they had devised with Athol Fugard, *Sizwe Bansi is Dead*. Asked by Kani to provide his identity number, an unsuspecting member of the audience invented one on the spot. 'I do not expect a white man to lie,' came the withering retort.

I was even given the opportunity to tread the boards myself, playing with the university dramatic society: Baptista in *The Taming of the Shrew*, wearing a costume hired from the Royal Shakespeare Company and bearing the name 'Roy Kinnear' on the label; Dame Chat in *Gammer Gurton's Needle*, my first excursion into drag; and Thomas à Becket in *Murder in the Cathedral*, delivering T. S. Eliot's mesmeric verse and stirring prose sermon. Having essayed a martyred saint, I was promoted to God in the medieval morality play, *Everyman*. I thought I could ascend no higher, but it was suggested that I direct a play, the ultimate omnipotence. I chose Eugène Ionesco's *Exit the King*, recruiting a powerful cast of student actors to perform a work that had haunted me since 1962 when I first saw it at the Royal Court in London with Sir Alec Guinness as Berenger, a disintegrating monarch who refuses to accept his own mortality. It is the only production I ever directed.

After eight years we left Scotland in 1978. I feared being stuck in a groove. Universities, which had been expanding so fast in the late 1960s and much of the following decade, were beginning to draw in their horns. The teaching of literature was becoming more theory based and so, in my opinion, less intelligible. Scotland, as it approached its first devolution referendum, was perhaps itself becoming less open to the internationalism which propelled my own academic work. I had a perfect illustration of this in Edinburgh, where I started a discussion group for schoolteachers to consider possible post-colonial texts to introduce to their pupils. I contacted teachers all round Scotland and most replied sympathetically, but one from Pitlochry wrote belligerently that there was absolutely no point in any of his children being taught African, Caribbean or Indian authors because – didn't I realise? – they lived in a place where there were no black or Asian residents and it would be completely irrelevant to their needs. I wrote back and said I thought his school was precisely the kind our campaign to widen the cultural syllabus was aimed at, but I had no reply.

These had been glorious years for us and we knew we were taking a risk by my giving up a tenured position and Helen a senior administrative role at the Open University in Edinburgh. I have returned to Scotland every year since. In the intervening decades I came to understand the case for Scottish independence as I did not when living there. A nation must feel at ease with itself. Paradoxically, Scotland may thereby return to the close intellectual and political affinity with Europe that has characterised its history from earliest times.

4

AFRICA AGAIN, THOUGH DIFFERENTLY: LONDON, 1970s and 1980s

A major part of my role at Stirling University had been to build up its profile in Commonwealth literary studies, or the 'new literatures' as they were sometimes termed. With historians on the staff who were equally committed to post-colonial discourse, especially two outstanding Africanists, Robin Law and John McCracken, it had been a highly stimulating enterprise across several areas of the university. Even Leeds did not at the time cover as much ground as we did at Stirling. We were the first university in the country to run specialist courses on Caribbean writing, Indian literature, and many aspects of African cultural and social development, let alone survey courses that crossed the Commonwealth comparatively. With Derry Jeffares leaving the Leeds ship to join ours, we became the leading department in Britain in a discipline that was fast evolving its own critical vocabulary and increasingly commanding global attention.

I had no planned intention of leaving the university sector, but I could not resist applying for the post of Director-General of the Africa Centre in London. It was a long shot. I was white for a start. I had no solid management experience, had never been responsible for a significant budget, and had only occasionally been in Africa since living there nine years before. Nor was I a Roman Catholic, though the Centre had been set up by public figures of Catholic provenance, including the Earl of Perth, the premier aristocrat in Scotland, and the politician Shirley Williams, who were assisted financially by the Cardinal Hinsley Trust and administratively by The Sword of the Spirit (later the Catholic Institute of International Relations and later still Progressio). Head-hunters had been sent out to search for a new Director-General to take over from Margaret Feeny, who had been in post since the Centre opened in 1964. She was a devout Catholic, bilingual in French and English, who had launched the Centre successfully and whose inexhaustible energy never dimmed. After interviews in Edinburgh and London I was appointed, taking up my post on 1st August 1978.

When I started work at the Africa Centre, which was based in Covent Garden, I was often reminded of the old Ivor Novello song, 'And Her Mother Came Too'. I had not appreciated that in succeeding Margaret, Margaret herself would be part of the package. She announced on my first morning that she would be retaining an office in the Centre, 'just in order to keep an eye on things'. It was a year or so before I had the confidence to take decisions on my own, at which point she began to fade out. She moved to Bath, where she became active in local politics and eventually mayor of the city. When she died in 2012 at the age of 94, I attended her memorial service at Corpus Christi Church in Covent Garden and was saddened to be in a congregation of barely thirty people – that for a woman who in her heyday was as well networked and widely admired as anyone I have ever known. I left the church in the company of Baroness Williams and we walked together back to the Africa Centre, one last visit for both of us and in spirit for Margaret, before the site was bought and re-developed in 2013.

The idea for an Africa Centre in central London had arisen from the growing number of African students in the capital, the increased West African population settling in Britain at large, and a perceived need to have a focal point on Africa as one by one its colonies moved to independence. President Kenneth Kaunda of Zambia had formally opened the Centre in 1964. His photograph presided in my office throughout my tenure and I was delighted that, on the one occasion I met him, he was waving his signature white handkerchief just as he was in the picture. The Centre occupied premises at 38 King Street, which had served many functions since the mid eighteenth century. Originally a showroom for a glass purveyor, it was later a book depository frequented by Samuel Johnson. From 1831 to 1939 it functioned as Stevens Auction Rooms, where aptly enough, given its African future, it was the setting for the sale of the last dodo's egg from Mauritius, shell collections from around the African continent, and the Benin Bronzes from what later became Nigeria. The tale of this period is told in an obscure book called *A Romance of the Rostrum*, by E. G. Allingham, a copy of which I was delighted to find amid a pile of rubbish in a cupboard (13). In the 1940s the building fell on hard times, becoming – shades of its African provenance again? – a banana warehouse overflowing from the nearby Covent Garden vegetable market. With ecclesiastical funders behind it, The Centre had been able to purchase the building, which meant that it was in a position thereafter to let out offices and derive its most stable income. In my time I brought in the International African Institute and, with the publisher Christopher Hurst, helped set up the Africa Book Centre, which acted as a shop window for Africa-related publications.

The Centre was open seven days a week. The weekends were mainly devoted to music and social gatherings. Great musicians such as Dollar Brand, Fela Kuti and Hugh Masekela began their London careers at the Centre. From Monday to Thursday it ran adult education classes and a programme of lectures and discussions. A typical day might start with the visit of a school party to hear about African development. A favourite exercise was to ask them to write a report on an economic crisis facing an invented African country. 'Azania depends almost entirely on the production of sugar for its income, but there has been a glut of sugar around the world because of health experts appealing for reduction in its use. Imagine you are a journalist and write a short report about this situation for *The Sun/Times/Guardian/Daily Mail/Financial Times/Morning Star*/BBC.' To familiarise them with various styles of media, the children would be given briefing material before they embarked on their interviews of role-playing staff. I might be the chairman of the national-ised sugar industry in Azania, the catering manager a sugar farmer, the education officer an underpaid work-er and the accountant a disgruntled tourist arriving at what he thought would be a tropical paradise, only to find it on its knees because of the collapse of the sugar trade. The teenager impersonating *The Sun* would come up with an inventive headline – *SUGAR SLUMPS!* The young man writing for *The Morning Star* would blame the crisis on western capitalism and the young woman representing *The Mail* might invent a tale on the lines of 'Sugar Insult: Royal Visit Cancelled'.

There would then be a frantic turn around before classes started – Swahili and Arabic, Shona and Amhar-ic, African Literature (which I often taught), African Drumming and African Dance (neither of which were easily compatible with anything else going on in the building, but we managed), Politics and Economics of Development, English as a Second Language, Africa Through Film, Afro-Caribbean History and Culture.

Courses came and went, but the tutors were all excellent and people enrolled because they could not find any other institution offering these specialisms.

It was a vibrant time for Africa and the Centre reflected it. Since the Gold Coast colony had become the independent republic of Ghana in 1956, there had been a steady process of decolonisation, in Francophone and Lusophone countries as well as Anglophone. There remained, however, huge issues still to be resolved. *Apartheid* in South Africa was firmly entrenched. The status of Rhodesia/Zimbabwe was not resolved until 1980. Conflicts seemed endemic in the Western Sahara, Eritrea, Zaire and other areas of the continent. There were also divergent views of how the 'Third World', as we then termed developing countries, should best move forward and what role western aid should play in this process. I look back to my first Annual Report for the Africa Centre, published in 1979, and am pleased to see how enthusiastic I was for the move I had made, which had not been without difficulty. My father-in-law, whom I much respected, worried greatly about the risk I had taken in giving up a tenured post and moving to a financially challenged charity. I expressed my belief in what I was doing thus:

After years of University life where it is not uncommon to hear practiced academics purveying worn-out lectures it is refreshing to be at an institution where every talk seems fresh and authoritative. (14)

I went on to write of the Centre's traditionally apolitical stance and to point out that we had run objectively focused discussions on topics such as 'Rhodesian Oil Sanctions, For and Against' and 'The Ethiopian Revolution: Two Interpretations'.

There was some ingenuousness in my claim that the Centre was neutral. It was, in the sense that it made a point of covering every part of the continent and in presenting different perspectives on most issues, but it could not possibly remain neutral towards such a moral outrage as *apartheid* or Ian Smith's Unilateral Declaration of Independence in Rhodesia. One needed only venture into the Centre's bar any evening to find it full of exiles from these countries. Most of them were yearning to be back home, and by the end of my time at the Centre a lot of the Zimbabweans had returned. I never doubted that Rhodesia would evolve into Zimbabwe, though I did not anticipate the monstrous violations of probity over which the new President, Robert Mugabe, would preside. We were all proud of the fact that his first wife, Sally Mugabe, who had she lived might have proved his saviour, was an employee of the Africa Centre until not long before I arrived.

I was no less pleased that Zimbabwe's most promising writer, Dambudzo Marechera, who in 1979 won *The Guardian* Fiction Prize for *The House of Hunger*, felt so at home at the Africa Centre. He had been thrown out of Oxford University and had come to London to make his way as a writer. He could be disarmingly charming. When we first met, he was dressed in a blue blazer with a tie. He was eager to please. Under his arm was a copy of Ezra Pound's *Cantos*, though on later occasions that was rather self-consciously replaced by George Orwell's *Down and Out in Paris and London*. He spoke with a cultivated posh accent, which was offset by a strong stammer that made one feel protective towards him, even whilst willing him to get his words out. I promised him whatever help we could give and invited him to think of the Centre as his home. He took me literally. He began sleeping on the premises and on many occasions he behaved outrageously.

One evening I was entertaining to dinner John Johnson, head of the Africa section of the Foreign and Commonwealth Office (FCO), who doubled as the London-based British Ambassador to Chad. John had given an engrossing talk about Chad, but I had an ulterior motive in having him as my guest. I wanted to persuade the FCO to start making an annual grant to the Africa Centre. It was vital that the evening should go well. We were dining in the middle of the Calabash, the Centre's excellent basement restaurant, which was looking its best. Our admirable head waiter, Atris Salem, who though functionally illiterate could commit to memory a complex order for any number of people, was on hand to ensure the best service. All was well until there was a sudden crash. Dambudzo had arrived, naked to the waist. He proceeded to prowl the perimeter of the restaurant, tipping up each table whether or not anyone was at it, so that whatever was on it slid to the floor. To his great credit, Johnson of the FO waved aside my apologies and continued to talk amiably as though nothing had happened. I was reminded of British troops in the Ashanti wars of the 1890s who would dress for dinner and toast Queen Victoria's health in champagne while nearby drums beat louder and the 'natives' closed in. Such *sangfroid* on his part and such embarrassment on mine! We never got our grant and for a while longer I meekly put up with Dambudzo's interruptions in the name of artistic integrity.

Then came a night when around 4 a.m. I received a 'phone call at home from the resident caretaker, Paolo Diop, who was also the Centre's chef. 'What should I do, please? Dambudzo is on the pavement outside smashing all our windows with bricks.' I implemented the only sanction I could think of, which was to ban him from ever entering the premises again. A day or two later I had a call from James Currey, the publisher of Heinemann's African Writers Series, in which of course *The House of Hunger* featured. 'I just think I should warn you, Alastair, that we have had to ban Dambudzo from entering Heinemann's building again. It's the first time the company has done this to one of its authors since we began in 1890.' To my amazement Dambudzo accepted both James's and my decisions. Not long after he returned to Zimbabwe, where sadly he died at age 35, ostensibly of HIV-AIDS. It is a tale of high talent wrecked by mental distress, anger, and an unsustainable lifestyle of drugs, drink, selling his body and challenging all authority. I felt what it must have been like to know Chatterton or young Dylan Thomas.

About South Africa it could be even bleaker. Slightly sad South African intellectuals such as Lewis Nkosi would regularly get drunk in our basement bar, biding their time until they might – it seemed a big 'might' at the time – return to their country in the dawn of its new freedom. We were aware that if we invited a prominent commentator on South African affairs, we almost certainly would have sitting in the audience a member of BOSS, the South African Security Agency, later replaced by the National Intelligence Service. He would most likely be in a dark grey suit, very blonde, and in every sense thick. One day walking up Tottenham Court Road I bumped into Alex La Guma, one of South Africa's best writers and a prominent member of the so-called Cape Coloured community. We chatted for a few minutes and passed on. A year later I met Alex again in London. He explained that our chance meeting a year before had nearly resulted in his application for permission to travel outside South Africa being turned down. I asked him why. He explained that he had been summoned to the permit office and shown a photograph of himself talking with me in Tottenham Court Road. In other words, he had been trailed on his previous visit and the authorities now wanted to know who he had been meeting for what they had decided was an arranged assignation. The South African spy network was clearly efficient to at least some degree.

This was the period when any self-respecting opponent of white minority rule in South Africa observed a boycott of South African produce or of banks with strong links to the country. If we heard of anyone planning to travel to South Africa we implored them to desist. If the flatulent answer came that it was necessary to see for oneself before one jumped to conclusions, or, even less convincingly after the visit had taken place, that one knew better because one had been there and really the South African government was much more benevolent than portrayed and the local black population actually rather happy and they all smiled and what's more loved music, and didn't you know that white people really looked after their servants who loved them in return, one came close to despair. How could anything fundamentally change if such blindness prevailed? Yet one never gave up hope that it would. People like Mike Terry, and the Anti-Apartheid Movement he led, came regularly to the Africa Centre. I was in awe of their resolve, courage and acumen.

Inch by inch the situation was changing. Certain moments stand out for me, such as a lunch with Cyril Ramaphosa. The Central Office of Information, which was in effect the government's hospitality section, used to bring African guests to the Centre as part of their itinerary while on official visits to the United Kingdom. They included foreign ministers, senior civil servants, prominent journalists, and trade union officials. Ramaphosa, who is now President of a free South Africa, was one of the latter, working for the Council of Unions of South Africa. We had a long lunch in the Calabash, during which he told me about some of the injustices gnawing on his country and his conviction that, even though he might not see them corrected in his lifetime, he was confident that a more equal South Africa would come about one day. He came across as a man of humility and integrity. There have been criticisms of him in the ensuing years, mainly of his business dealings, which have made him a rand billionaire, but I hang on to a conviction formed that day. 'If only a man like that could run South Africa,' I said to colleagues after lunch. Well, that is what he is doing now.

Some of the most articulate representations of South Africa's predicament came to the Centre in the form of plays. The black South African playwright Matsemela Manaka, who was to die in a car crash in 1998, brought several productions to the Centre and explained to me that these had first been performed in townships, advertised only by word of mouth but huge in their impact. No scripts were published and by the time the authorities had caught up with the fact that the play had been put on, Matsemela's Soyikwa African Theatre Company had moved on. There was no evidence for a prosecution or a ban. Theatre had a significant surreptitious role in the struggle against *apartheid*, and not just through underground companies like Soyikwa. I persuaded the great white South African actress Yvonne Bryceland, who had created several of Athol Fugard's principal roles and who was at the time playing leads at the National Theatre across the river from the Centre, to perform for free a one-woman play, *Miss South Africa* (6), by Barney Simon. This powerful piece depicted the neurosis of a white beauty queen, yearning for praise, but terrified of the world encompassing her.

Without wings or a dressing room, staging drama at the Africa Centre was a fraught business, but in my years there nearly sixty plays were put on. Each one threw a light on Africa or its diaspora that, at the time, was shining hardly anywhere else. Though conditions for staging were technically minimal, there was continuing demand from new directors and fringe companies to perform. My first visit to the Centre, two years before my appointment, was to see *The Trials of Brother Jero*, an early work by Wole Soyinka. In the week I began working there, Theatre of Contemporary Arabic Drama put on *The New Arrival*, a play by Mikhail Roman, who despite his name was Egyptian. As I left the Centre six years later Ngũgĩ wa Thiong'o, the Kenyan writer formerly known as James Ngũgĩ, was in residence staging his epic play, *The Trial of Dedan Kimathi*, co-written with Micere Githae Mugo. It made a great impact and went on to tour successfully.

Dedan Kimathi was, of course, a Mau Mau leader. He was executed in 1957 by the British rulers of Kenya. He exemplified the adage that one man's terrorist is another's freedom fighter. I did not doubt the efficacy of putting on a play which extolled him, especially one written and directed by Ngũgĩ, who by now was a world-famous writer in contention for the Nobel Prize. I ran a risk in doing so, however, because there was always at the Africa Centre a balance to maintain between its radical programme and its 'establishment' and Christian provenance. One of the most satisfying innovations in my time was to start an art gallery. The wrought iron balcony which went round every side of the main hall lent itself perfectly to displaying paintings and photographs. In 1982 we curated an exhibition called 'Roots in Britain', which focused on the lives of black and Asian people in England from Elizabeth I to Elizabeth II. There was a portrait included of the present Queen, depicting her as a vampire with blood oozing from her mouth. I did not like the painting, nor did I fully share its implicit critique of ravenous British imperialism feeding on the peoples it had colonised. The Centre's Treasurer, Sir Philip de Zulueta, who had been Private Secretary to three Conservative Prime Ministers (Anthony Eden, Harold Macmillan and Alec Douglas-Home), took much greater exception to it and demanded that it be taken down. It duly was, but for no more than 24 hours when it was quietly put back.

We had an effective governing body, but incidents like this made me grateful that I usually knew when they would be coming to the Centre so that I could remove incriminating evidence. Our Chairman for my first four years was Chief Emeka Anyaoku, the Commonwealth Deputy Secretary-General. A Nigerian diplomat of immense intelligence and charm, he kept a watchful eye on us, but did not interfere. He stepped down in July 1982, briefly in the following year becoming Nigeria's Foreign Minister before he returned to London to resume his Commonwealth role, prior to assuming the Commonwealth Secretary-Generalship itself in 1990, a post he held with distinction for ten years. He and his wife Bunmi were always kind to us, but I understood that he would not let sentiment stand in the way if I were to misdirect the Centre. Six years after I left it, I was his guest at his home in Obosi, eastern Nigeria, where a decade earlier he had been installed as the Ichie Adazie, a senior chief. He was about to take up the top Commonwealth post and was preparing himself for it, so devoting time to me was a gesture I enormously valued. Apart from those he employed, there were only the two of us in his home for the few days I was there, but it was a momentous week as Nelson Mandela was about to be released after his long incarceration. Emeka would break off from our chats to take calls from round the world. I was not, of course, privy to their content, but there was no doubting the gravity as well as the joy of this historic moment. He confessed to me his greatest anxiety: that something violent would happen to Mandela as he stepped out of prison, as it had done when in 1983 the Filipino politician Benigno Aquino returned from exile and was assassinated as he emerged from his flight.

Chief Anyaoku's successor as Chairman of the Centre was Thomas Okelo-Odongo, Secretary-General of the Africa-Caribbean-Pacific Agency in Brussels. On paper he fitted the bill perfectly, being Kenyan and head of the main consortium of developing countries liaising with the European Economic Community, but in practice he was ineffective. However, there were astute and experienced members on the Council of Management, who ensured its good governance, among them Lord Perth, the only one of the Centre's founders still to be involved; Anthony Allott, professor of African Law at the School of Oriental and African Studies (SOAS); George Bennett, head of the BBC African Service; Margaret Busby, the publisher; Buchi Emecheta, the writer; and Kaye Whiteman, editor of the influential, though now defunct, journal *West Africa*. Sir Philip de Zulueta arrived at the Centre one evening for a small finance meeting – there were only four of us present and the business was routine. 'I've stood up Mrs. Thatcher to be here,' he said. He explained that the Prime Minister had invited him to dinner, but he had declined because of his commitment to our meeting. I asked why on earth he had given priority to the Centre. 'If I have an appointment in my diary, then I am honour bound to keep it, no matter what it is. Otherwise I would be letting people down.' It is counsel I have tried to live by ever since, though probably not as rigorously observed as it was by that admirable man.

I had a hard-working team of colleagues, who were not afraid of speaking their minds. I had only been six months at the Centre when several of them came to see me and explained that, though I appeared to be a nice enough person, I had not imparted any vision to them of the direction I wanted the organisation to take. It was a huge wake-up call. I realised that being pleasant and enthusiastic were not sufficient to make for good management. Small matters like three-year business plans, strategic vision, risk registers and mission statements were also expected of me. Fortunately, while I matured into my post, these colleagues held the fort brilliantly. I look back with great satisfaction to working with Wendy Davies, Paolo Diop, Nawal Domun, Tony Humphries, Patrick Kankya, Murray McCartney, Ben Nganda, Susan Odamtten, Tunde Oderinde, and many others. Several of them remain friends.

Murray and his wife, Irene Staunton, whom he met at the Africa Centre, run Weaver Press, a publishing company which vigorously keeps alive the spirit of free expression in Zimbabwe. I have stayed with them in Harare several times. In later years I visited Paolo and his wife Marie in Senegal, where he was running his own restaurant and she was a senior adviser to the President. Paolo had been a superb chef at the Africa Centre and often cooked for diplomats, including Chief Anyaoku; now he showed me around the small town of M'bour where he had settled. He took me into his local church and sat quietly in the seat at the front which he used at Mass every day. I could not believe it when I heard that this charming, talented and fit-looking man had succumbed to cancer only a year later.

There were two flies in the ointment. A catering manager whom we employed for some time turned out to be an embezzler and thief. He pleaded guilty on the day the case reached court. More difficult to handle was an Ethiopian colleague, Alem Mezgebe, who was taken on as a programme organiser, but who pleased himself as to what that programme might comprise and whether it required him to come to work. An intellectual and gifted man, his non-compliance eventually became too unjust for his colleagues to bear, let alone me.

After due warning, he was asked to leave. He had up to a year in which he could appeal to an industrial tribunal. On the 365th day of that year he took up this option, claiming among other grievances racial discrimination by me and the Council, the only occasion in my years at the Centre that my white skin was used against me. I was well advised by Professor Allott and others with the interests of the Centre at heart and we won the case. Alem's chances of winning had vanished when he tried to justify to the court why he was so often absent from his desk. He claimed to be out and about working for the Centre, citing as an example a day on which he said he was at London airport awaiting the arrival of a distinguished guest. I was able to check the veracity of this in time to present to the tribunal a copy of the letter which this guest had written to me some weeks earlier, regretting that he would be unable to come to Britain as planned because of changed circumstances. Where Alem Mezgebe actually was that day I do not know, but it is unlikely to have been Heathrow.

Apart from the blessed fact that we owned the building we occupied, with consequent rents from tenants, the Centre had no secure income. Small grants trickled in from a few corporate companies and a handful of African governments; the British government's subvention was axed within a week of Thatcher's election in 1979. I often wondered how that could have been a priority for a new administration dedicated to turning around the whole of society, and it was hard not to see an element of racism in it. Much of my time was spent fund-raising, with mixed success. I feared at times for the survival of the Centre and wondered where the next month's salaries would come from. There was a small patch of land in Floral Street which we sold for a sum that kept us going until the core income improved, but it was always touch and go. Occasional fund-raising forays to Africa on behalf of the Centre were never as productive as I hoped, though a visit to Kenya allowed Helen and me, after my business appointments in Nairobi with ministers and corporate executives, to travel north to Garissa. We did this journey on a public mini 'bus, accompanied all the way by armed soldiers in case of attack by the 'shifters', gangs who in another century would have been called highwaymen.

Sometimes the British Council would ask me to give lectures in Africa, and I would take advantage of a trip not costing the Africa Centre anything to do what I could to raise money for it. It was not easy. In 1981 I embarked on such a visit to Ghana, my first time back since living there. On arrival I learned that all the universities had gone on strike. I spent a delightful fortnight as guest of the Council's Representative, Warren Shaw, but did not give a single talk or, sadly, secure any money for the Centre. I did, however, have the privilege of an audience at his palace in Kumasi with the Asantehene, Opoku Ware II, king of the Ashantis.

On this occasion I went on from Ghana to Liberia, where I was guest of the British Ambassador. Tony Allott, a congenial member of the Centre's Council who had advised me over the Mezgebe problem, was also there as an old friend of the family. In the nineteenth century Britain had been rewarded by the Liberian government for its early recognition of the nation's free status with a gift of the finest land in the centre of Monrovia, on a promontory on the edge of the sea, with a spectacular outlook. There our embassy was situated until a few years after my stay. Again, however, though I gave a lecture, I raised little money. It was unrealistic to ask a developing economy to donate to an institution in the heart of one of the world's great financial centres.

Liberia was peaceful when I was there, but only the year before President Tolbert had been murdered in a *coup d'état*. The first formal luncheon Helen and I ever attended in London was in honour of Tolbert when he made an official visit, so we had rued his bloody end. We had been apprehensive about how we should behave at such a formal occasion, which was held at the Mansion House and was packed with City dignitaries and business leaders. It had not gone well because the waitress managed to pour gravy from the roast lamb down the back of Helen's dress. She remained greasily uncomfortable as she struggled to look rapt and unconcerned during the speeches. Tolbert's predecessor as President, William Tubman, had a nephew in London, to whom I was able to tell the sorry tale of Helen's ruined dress. He was an amiable man, who rejoiced in the name Winston Adolf Tubman. His family had been hedging their bets when he was born in 1941.

The Centre's financial worries were debilitating enough, but I was also burning the candle at both ends.

I began to wonder what I might do next, but not before taking stock of what had been achieved. After six years I felt I could point to a successful institution that punched above its weight. We had developed partnerships with kindred organisations such as the Commonwealth Institute. We had put on over a hundred lectures a year in addition to our educational and cultural programme. Major African writers had given readings or talks – not only Achebe and Ngũgĩ, but Elechi Amadi, Dennis Brutus, Buchi Emecheta (an active member of the Centre's governing body and a vibrant contributor to our constant focusing on African feminism), Nuruddin Farah, Bessie Head, Jack Mapanje, Njabulo Ndebele, Flora Nwapa, Gabriel Okara, Ben Okri, Sembène Ousmane, Amos Tutuola, and Wole Soyinka, to say nothing of C. L. R. James, Naomi Mitchison, Samuel Selvon, and many other authors with invaluable reflections on human rights and international development. We devised several major book exhibitions, including Bookweek Africa in 1982, the most ambitious display of publications from Africa ever to be seen in Britain. It followed a specialist exhibition the previous year of Zimbabwean literature, a revelation to many who only thought of that country in terms of war and racism.

Not long after my arrival the Africa Centre had opened an art gallery where painters and craftspeople of repute exhibited, including Tayo Adenaike, Sokari Douglas Camp, Ablade Glover, Seyni Diagne Diop, Bruce Onokbrakpeya, and the great soapstone sculptors of Zimbabwe, such as Sylvester Mubayi, whose works signify in the international art market today. Under the title *Lost Heritage*, we arranged a major UNESCO funded symposium on the return of cultural property. David Wilson, Director of the British Museum, had previously declined all invitations to speak on this fraught topic but bravely agreed to do so at the Centre. He defended what many critics saw as cultural appropriation by saying that it was vital to have the means of conserving artefacts, which was not always the case in developing countries where power failures were frequent. He also unapologetically said that his museum's policy was to display originals, not copies. He was Daniel in the lion's den, but rather magnificently so. When invited by one of the delegates, Charles Mungo from the Commonwealth Arts Association, to defend the Museum from the charge of arrogance for daring to assume that it was 'better able to "hold in trust" objects of vital importance to people, better, that is, than they themselves can hold these items,' Wilson responded:

The word 'arrogance' is an emotive word. I will not be arrogant in my statement, but I think I should answer the last speaker. The experience of the British Museum is that it has managed for a very long time to keep the collection which it has in its charge and although in not every case has it been kept perfectly, there is no other museum in the world which has a better record. (15)

Such moments truly resonated. Indeed, if any government minister or visiting dignitary from Africa had something important to say about the continent, it was probable they would seek to say it at the Africa Centre. Journalists were taking note of what went on there.

I revelled in all this activity, loved the Calabash's food (especially the *egusi*, which mixed meat and fish in a very unEuropean way), and would even sometimes step gingerly onto the dance floor to join in a Ghanaian highlife or to clap along a visiting jazz group. Led by one of our regular musicians, Emmanuel Josiah, we played music on the pavement of King Street the day the Covent Garden vegetable market closed, until the police came along and humourlessly moved us on for blocking the way. I wrote a letter of complaint about it.

Much of this endless activity was great fun. All of it was interesting. I was also quite status conscious, so the idea of giving up the impressive title 'Director-General' bothered me. It secured me invitations to government lunches, appearances on BBC radio, and national day celebrations at embassies and high commissions. I was waiting for a big opportunity to unfold in front of me, but I waited in vain. Life rarely works to such a plan.

Our personal lives were moving on too. On leaving Scotland, we moved to Berkhamsted for four years, to a spacious Victorian house beside the Grand Union canal. This was in order to be equi-distant from London, to which I commuted daily, and the headquarters of the Open University in Milton Keynes, where Helen had transferred. She had new demanding responsibilities of her own. However, having lived for some years with the disappointment of not having a baby, we set about the arduous process of seeking to adopt one. The adoption agency kept likening the process to a natural pregnancy; if so, we must have come close to setting a world record for gestation. At one stage, having been accepted as suitable candidates, we were told that there were no babies or young children available so we were being dropped from the list. Our compliance with the slightly patronising tone of the assessors imploded into real anger. We wrote to say that what was being done to us was the equivalent of a forced abortion after a full-term pregnancy. It did the trick and within a very short time we were asked if we would like to take on the most beautiful six-week old girl in the universe. Thus in 1981 Isabella Margaret Donna Niven became part of our family. She was followed in 1985 by another six-week old, Alexander Nigel William Niven. Two perfect children at the centre of our lives ever since.

The emotional strain on both of us was considerable. Though Helen took maternity leave and I did my best to be a good father, life was as tough for us as for any new parents. The commuting was increasingly problematic, especially in the cold winters we had at that time and with the rail network trying to cope with the fragmentising aftermath of privatisation, leading to long delays. We decided to move to what we thought would be a more manageable house on a modern estate in Milton Keynes Village, a small but ancient community which, to defuse jealousy from Bletchley, Stony Stratford and Wolverton, had given its name to Britain's newest town. We did not choose wisely. Our house had little character and we were dependent on driving everywhere. To make life more difficult, but also to ensure that I kept abreast of my specialism, I accepted invitations to lecture for the British Council abroad or attend international literary conferences. This meant that I was often away. Fortunately I was with Helen when her father died suddenly before our eyes one hot July evening in 1983 just as we arrived for the weekend.

I had sufficiently heeded my father-in-law's concerns about abandoning the safe embrace of a tenured position in 1978 to approach SOAS to see if my services might be useful there. Two members of the School were sure they could be: Gordon Innes, professor of West African Languages, and B. W. 'Goosh' Andrzejewski, the great Somali scholar credited for having been the first person to script the Somali language. I was invited to accept an honorary lectureship, giving me access to London University's facilities and allowing me to continue using an academic designation, in return for which I would introduce the teaching of African literature in English. This was done within an M.A. programme called Area Studies (Africa).

I began at SOAS in 1979 with two students and ended five years later with sixteen. Preparing for the classes and marking essays was a big extra commitment, but I enjoyed the stimulus. I was not paid for this work, which had been part of the agreement when I was taken on, but I began to think that as a matter of self-respect I should be given some kind of honorarium. I wrote to the Principal of the School, Jeremy Cowan, asking in mild language if consideration could be given to my case for pecuniary recognition, however modest. I could not believe his reply, one of the rudest letters I have ever received. Professor Cowan told me that I should consider myself fortunate to work at such a distinguished institution as SOAS (which I knew I was) and if I wished to go elsewhere that was fine by him. There was no mention of my teaching, of the numbers my course attracted to the School, or of the benefit which the School received from being linked to the Africa Centre. I felt I had no option but to resign my position. The School was left with a commitment to my ongoing students and those registering for the following year. As a result, it had to create from scratch a lectureship in African literature in English, with a salary of around £25,000. I would have accepted a tenth of that.

I not only resigned from SOAS in 1984, but made good my resolution to move on from the Africa Centre. It was one of the riskiest decisions of my life. My salary there was never high, but it was a steady income. Now we would have to rely only on Helen's salary or on any freelance fees I could earn. I have often wondered if I would have had the nerve to carry through my determination to resign if Helen's father had still been alive. He would immediately have seen the burden being placed on Helen, at a time when we were hoping for a second child. Being part of that generation which in the 1930s had known what unemployment meant, he would have been fearful for all our futures.

I loved my years at the Africa Centre, fraught though they were by money worries, but I knew I had come to the end of the road creatively. Looking back, I am confident that almost everything moved forward under my direction and that the Centre's dedication to African development was every bit as strong as it had been under Margaret Feeny. But I was physically as well as mentally tired. I departed in the summer of 1984, knowing that I would be well succeeded by Nigel Watt, General Secretary of International Voluntary Service. Africa would always be central to my life, but I would no longer feel that I was carrying the whole weight of the continent upon my shoulders, as, absurdly but truthfully, it had often seemed in these eclectic years.

5

COMMONWEALTH, 1980s

The Commonwealth has never been well understood in Britain. Every year on the second Monday of March, which is Commonwealth Day, it is celebrated at an impressive service in Westminster Abbey, to which I have often been invited. The Queen, as Head of the Commonwealth, is almost always there – though there has been one exception to which I will allude later. The Prime Minister, the Commonwealth Secretary-General, religious representatives, High Commissioners and chief executives of appropriate charities also attend. Actors, choirs, steel bands and sports personalities perform or deliver upbeat homilies. Most impressively, there is a parade of national flags of the 53 member countries, carried by young people and led by the Commonwealth's own flag. Children from schools around the U.K. are a substantial part of the congregation, occupying the nave from the Unknown Warrior's grave to the choir stalls. A Martian dropping in on the Commonwealth Observance, as it is sometimes termed, might form the impression that this organisation is the kernel of British life. It is not. British governments over the years have blown hot and cold about it, always paying it lip service but in practice often either ignoring it or, worse in some ways, regarding it as a grouping which can be played as a useful counter to Europe whenever they are in Brexit mode. It is still not unusual to hear it referred to as the British Commonwealth, though 'British' was dropped from its designation in the London Declaration of April 1949. A sentimental view prevails among some MPs and commentators that the U.K.'s problems would be solved if we could only re-kindle the spirit that once brought us butter mountains from New Zealand, soldiers when we needed them from Australia, and nice white settlers disenchanted with the new South Africa and Zimbabwe. History does not move backwards.

I doubt very much if the average British child, unless privileged to have been among the lucky few at an annual gathering in Westminster, would have much cogent to say about how the Commonwealth functions. The man or woman in the street is even more ignorant, apart from knowing that the Commonwealth is dear to Her Majesty. I have often been asked if it has any point in the twenty-first century, if it really exists, or if it will quietly fold when there is a change of Headship. For all the cynicism surrounding it, I remain a great supporter of the Commonwealth concept and know from various attachments and links I have had with it over the years that it is a much more practical organisation than most people credit it with being. In my second chapter I quoted Gonzalo's utopian vision in *The Tempest*, in the name of 'commonwealth'. His ideal of a society free from exploitation and ruled by natural justice seems to me as viable an aspiration in my eighth decade as it was when I went out to Ghana in 1966 to meet the developing world head-on for the first time. I have always been heartened by the play on words implicit in 'common wealth' and inspired by the radical connections of the term, which was Oliver Cromwell's way of describing this realm in the mid-seventeenth century, and which Australia adopted in 1901 to express its self-determination, and which Kentucky, Massachusetts, Pennsylvania and Virginia used even before they were fully admitted to the United States.

Much of my work at the Africa Centre inevitably focused on Commonwealth countries, though I ensured that attention was also paid to *La Francophonie*, the Maghreb, Lusofonia and the Horn of Africa. The then flourishing Commonwealth Institute in Kensington, with its superb modern architecture and versatile exhibition space, became one of our close partners. Indeed I was part of its Working Party on Commonwealth Literature and Library Holdings, put together by its Librarian Michael Foster, which helped build up the Institute's excellent resource centre and did much to promote wider knowledge of Commonwealth authors.

In 1979, shortly after I joined the Africa Centre, I took on co-editorship of *The Journal of Commonwealth Literature*, considered by many to be the leading academic journal in its field. Andrew Gurr and later Angus Calder were the other co-editors and I worked very closely with the quirky but remorsely hard-working Hans Zell as our publisher. He and his colleague Mary Jay held us to tight deadlines and fastidious editorial standards, from which I knew I sometimes fell short. Articles were submitted from all round the world. Selecting the few that could be published and editing them meticulously was a time-consuming process, but we maintained standards we had inherited from the journal's founding editor Arthur Ravenscroft. One issue a year was devoted entirely to bibliographies of recent publications from around the Commonwealth. The best of our compilers, such as Shyamala Narayan, who covered India, or Dorothy Driver from South Africa, were beyond praise in their precision and breadth.

As I moved into the 1980s, commitment to Commonwealth initiatives increasingly became central to my life. I was associated in its final years with the Commonwealth Poetry Prize, and in 1987 I edited an anthology of its winning entries from 1972, when it began, to 1986, shortly before its demise through lack of sponsorship. Chinua Achebe from Nigeria and George McWhirter, an Ulster-born Canadian, were its first joint winners. The anthology took its title, *Under Another Sky*, from a poem, 'Epilogue', by Guyanese poet Grace Nichols, who won the prize in 1983, and who ever since has been a good friend.

> I have crossed an ocean
> I have lost a tongue
> from the root of the old one
> a new one has sprung (16)

Our inability to raise enough money to keep the award afloat, after years in which first the Diamond Corporation, then British Airways, and finally Dillon's Bookshop had supported it, was a salutary lesson to me in the hardship of running a creative enterprise, however worthy. I did not forget this in the years that followed when I was in the position of assigning funds, rather than begging for them.

In the same period, I developed my links with ACLALS, becoming its international secretary for several years. I went to its fifth triennial conference at the University of the South Pacific. I flew to Fiji on 31st December 1979. We arrived there on 2nd January 1980, the start of a new decade. On the flight we celebrated New Year with champagne three times as we crossed various date lines and time zones but we never experienced New Year's Day. My journal entry for Sunday 1st January 1980 consists of two words. 'Didn't exist'. The conference itself was one of the first of its kind to focus on comparative multi-culturalism; it was here that I first met Australia's great writers Les Murray and Kath Walker, later to be better known by her Aboriginal name Oodgeroo Noonuccal. Aside from its academic value, however, the conference threw up divisions within the Commonwealth community which even today are sometimes not fully acknowledged: the gulf between the 'haves' who, despite their good intentions towards developing peoples, want to go on having, and the 'have nots'. The accommodation for most participants was in student rooms on the university campus, which before the foundation of the university in 1968 had been an Air New Zealand site. Conditions, I recorded in my journal, were 'pokey'. Consequently, many of the delegates moved to smarter places in the centre of Suva. As I noted, slightly self-righteously perhaps, but with conviction, 'I feel strongly that it insults the organisers to go. One cannot profess an interest in Third World writing whilst boycotting the odd cockroach and uncomfortable bed. Yet about half the conference has moved to expensive downtown hotels'.

When the conference was over, I moved on to the island of Taveuni, third largest in the Fijian archipelago, where I stayed in a small hotel by myself. One afternoon I went for a walk along the coast of this palmfringed paradise. It was very hot so when I came to a quiet cove, with no one about, I stripped off and went for a swim. On returning to the hotel I said what I had been doing. 'Oh my God!' came the response from the manager. 'We should have warned you. At exactly that spot last week a local woman was wading knee-deep in the sea and a shark came and bit off both her legs.' Apparently it had been attracted by panniers of fish which the woman had strapped to her waist. I thought Taveuni possibly the most beautiful place I had ever visited and swore I would return one day with Helen. In 1990 I did so, with our young children. We slept in hammocks on the beach with the water lapping a metre away, but I made sure that none of us went on impromptu skinny dips without seeking local advice first.

I have continued to give papers on aspects of Commonwealth or post-colonial literature up to the present, usually under the auspices of ACLALS, or the British Council, or a host university. My best opportunity to talk about Shakespeare in a post-colonial context was sprung on me in the fading clapboard elegance of Georgetown, Guyana, when I was there as a judge of the Guyana Literature Prize. I had less than a day's notice and expected few people to be at the National Library when I arrived. It was packed with one of the most erudite and appreciative audiences I have ever addressed. The next day I was able to see the great Brian Lara play cricket for Trinidad against Guyana. I supported the home side, partly because I watched in the company of its cricketing legend, Joe Solomon.

In the 1980s and 1990s I visited many Commonwealth countries for the first time, giving academic talks: Australia, Canada, Malta, Singapore, Sri Lanka, and several more. My first of many stays in Australia was in 1982, on the occasion of the Commonwealth Games being held in Brisbane. For the first time it was decided to hold a cultural festival alongside the sport. I was asked to go with the poet Peter Porter as the official British participants in the writers' week that formed part of the event. Peter was Australian but lived in London, a wry and erudite commentator whose complex relationship with both countries was balanced by a calming devotion to music and language.

> Sailing away from ourselves, we feel
> The gentle tug of water at the quay –
> Language of the liberal dead speaks
> From the soil of Highgate, tears
> Show a great water table is intact.
> You cannot leave England, it turns
> A planet majestically in the mind. (17)

As part of the cultural programme an exhibition of Commonwealth costumes had been put together by the Nigerian all-rounder Jumoke Debayo. Jumoke realised shortly before the exhibition left England that it lacked one of the most distinctive examples of Commonwealth national dress, the kilt. I offered mine and it duly went to Australia for several months, though I suspect that Jumoke asked other Scottish friends if they could help because in the end there were about four kilts on display, the others rather grander than mine.

Canada allowed me to fulfil a theatrical ambition by going to the Shaw Theatre at Niagara, where I saw the Falls in full spate and satisfied my obscurantist obsession with forgotten plays by seeing Shaw's late comedy *The Simpleton of the Unexpected Isle.* Years later I was to work closely with the greatest Shaw scholar of our time, Michael Holroyd, and was delighted to lend him my copy of the programme for that production as he wrote his magnificent biography. I also went to the theatre in Stratford, Ontario, where Brian Bedford performed a near definitive Richard II.

In Malta we were received by the President of the Republic, Anton Buttigieg, himself a notable poet. Daniel Massa, at the time head of English at the University, welcomed his guests with a tour of the splendid Grand Harbour. He had memories of the siege of Malta in World War II, when cats were eaten and most of the supply ships sent to rescue islanders were torpedoed. In 2016 I was the guest speaker at a *festschrift* gathering for Dan's 80th birthday. Britain had just voted to leave the European Union, but there on the platform in the historic National Library in Valletta were the flags of Malta and the European Union. It was proudly pointed out that the Maltese Prime Minister, Joseph Muscat, was the current Commonwealth Chair-in-Office as well as the incoming President of the Council of the EU, tangible evidence if it were needed that commitment to both organisations was perfectly possible.

My first visit to Singapore, in 1987, was for a literature conference. The visit was marred for me by unexpected news from home. My father, aged 77, had been taken into hospital and, as a result of a blockage to the blood supply in his right leg, which threatened to turn gangrenous, had an amputation. He was the kind of man who made the whole world know if he had a cold, but his bravery in facing this disaster and later in learning to walk again with a prosthesis was remarkable. It was perhaps the start of a gradual process of feeling more sympathetic towards him and not allowing my tough memories of his shouting and absences when I was growing up to colour all my thoughts about him.

The main ACLALS conference in 1995 took place in Colombo. The Sri Lankan civil war was still disrupting the country and many people cried off the event. I wondered in hindsight whether I had been wise to go because the week after my return I read that the bank where I had changed travellers' cheques before leaving had been blown up with some loss of life. I would not, however, have missed the chance to climb Sigiriya, a rock 200 metres high on which King Kashyapa had built his fortified palace around 477 AD. I have no head for heights and found the clamber up the iron staircase on the sheer side of the rock dizzying. I was about to turn back when some Australians ahead of me, who had been at the same conference as I had, did exactly that. 'Too steep, mate!' they said. Since they had been goading the Poms throughout, I felt no alternative but to battle on to the top, averting my eyes from the drop below. 'Just good old Pommy determination!' I explained to them that evening.

At another conference in Colombo a few years later, the novelist Charlotte Cory was one of our number. She had discovered a diary, dated 1860, in a bookshop in Chester written by Lora Wilkinson, teenage daughter of the governor of Colombo. Charlotte gave a talk about the diary and asked someone in the audience to name any day of the year so that she could read out Lora's entry for that date. The entry described an ordinary morning in which Lora had gone riding up the Strand 'in the company of Tommy Rust', a boy a bit younger than herself. After her talk a shy Sri Lankan woman came up to Charlotte and told her that there was still a Miss Rust, an elderly lady, living near Kandy; she wondered if she might be a descendant. Charlotte determined to find out by visiting Miss Rust and asked me to accompany her for safety. We took the train to Kandy and enquired where a Miss Rust might live. The railway stationmaster turned out also to be the local historian. He invited us into his office, explaining that this had been Leonard Woolf's office too when he was in Ceylon around 1910. Yes, he knew a Miss Rust. She lived a quiet life some miles outside of Kandy. He found a car for us and off Charlotte and I went. We came to a large plantation house that had clearly seen better days. We prowled round it trying to attract someone's attention. Inside was a Sri Lankan family cooking; they told us that Miss Rust lived in a cottage at the bottom of the garden. We duly crossed what once must have been a lawn and knocked at the door. A man answered and, after we had explained our mission, showed us in. There we met Miss Rust, who was in her mid-eighties. The room was adorned with Union Jack bunting and she was surrounded by photographs of The Queen, Princess Diana and Winston Churchill. She had been brought up in the big house when her father ran the estate, she explained, but it had fallen on hard times. She had been to England once, in the 1920s;

however, she knew nothing of Tommy Rust. We decided that it had been a bizarre and interesting visit, with the decline of Empire made manifest before our eyes, and rose to say our goodbyes. On the way out we spied a wedding photograph on the hall table; on the back it was dated 1880 and, peering closer, we could make out that the groom was one Tommy Rust. Charlotte had found her answer. A few years later she published her book about Lora, *Imperial Quadrille*.

Given the nature of my specialism, my academic invitations were mainly in the Commonwealth, but I was fortunate enough also to be asked to various non-Anglophone countries to give talks. I felt very sorry for the director of the British Council in Belgium, who had to endure my lecture on 'Why D. H. Lawrence Went Abroad' many times as we moved from Liège to Louvain and across the border to Luxembourg. A highlight was my visit to Indonesia in 1985. Although it is the largest Muslim country in the world, the visit was centred on Manado, a city in the north of Sulawesi with a predominantly Roman Catholic population. I taught several classes whilst there for a week. The deprived educational resources in the university were shocking. One of the set books was George Orwell's *Animal Farm*, and I was happy to re-engage with a novel I had admired since my school days, but I had never expected to face a class with only part of the text available, and that in a tattered copy which had to be run off on an unreliable photocopier if one wanted to share it with more than one person. My Indonesian colleagues and hosts were, however, warmly welcoming and appreciative. I shall never forget the lunch given in my honour by a gracious Indonesian lady. As I surveyed a table groaning with unknown delicacies, she asked me to take the first helping. I asked about the choice. 'We have rat and bat and dog,' she replied. It was a dilemma and I was not quick enough to say that actually I had converted to vegetarianism in the last five minutes. I chose dog. My family have never forgiven me.

This miscellany of activities at home and abroad may have been a bravado front for being unsure of where my professional life was heading. I had left the Africa Centre in 1984 with no clear path ahead and launched myself as a freelancer, assembling what is today called a 'portfolio' of undertakings. I accepted anything that came my way. Much of it was fascinating and some of it was a privilege. I relied on what by then was a large network of contacts, but I quickly found, as though I did not know it already, that I was hopeless at selling myself or at hustling for commissions. Bluntly, not enough came my way to sustain an income. I also realised almost immediately that I was an institutional person. I needed to identify with an organisation, not just to project myself; to go into a building each morning and sit at an office desk, not merely move from the breakfast to the dining room table; to greet colleagues, not just my family and the cat. Mercifully, opportunities for work did not completely dry up.

One of these arose at the University of Buckingham. This at the time was the only fully independent 'privatised' university in the country. Arthur Pollard had moved there from the University of Hull, where I had been his external examiner. A notorious contributor to the 'Black Paper' on higher education in 1969, in private he belied his hard-right reputation by being utterly amiable. My visiting post was for less than a year, but I enjoyed both the teaching, many of the students being from overseas, and the ambiance of this small well-run institution. Driving there from Woburn Sands, skirting Milton Keynes, always delighted me.

Hull was one of many universities at which over the years I have been an external examiner of undergraduates. They also included Exeter, Kent, the South Bank, Moray House and Queen Margaret in Edinburgh, and Makerere in Uganda. Such opportunities became for my first year away from the Africa Centre one of my few ways of earning money. From time to time I was also asked to assess doctoral and master's theses in a wide range of institutions, not always pleasurably. My own doctorate may have been awarded for bulk as much as for quality, but at least it provided plenty of evidence that I had read a lot. It seemed to me that dissertations were not only getting more clogged with unintelligible theory but that they were also thinner. When I examined for Ph. D. an analysis of Patrick White, I asked the candidate why she had merely written on two of his fourteen novels, to say nothing of his short stories, plays and essays. She responded quite aggressively that her task was to focus in detail only on *Voss* and *The Tree of Man*. 'Might it not have been an idea, since you are aspiring to call yourself Doctor X for the rest of your life, at least to allude to some other works,' I ventured, 'if only to indicate context?' 'That would have been irrelevant,' she replied with finality. She did not get the degree, but I knew that many with similar views probably would.

Despite some disillusionment with higher education at the time, I still found the company of academics more often stimulating than not. I was keen, if possible, to retain my links with London University. Unbeknown to me my disagreement with the Principal of SOAS had reached the ears of some of my colleagues there, who thought I had been dealt with unjustly. Out of the blue came an invitation to join the Institute of Commonwealth Studies, which was housed almost next door. Its Director was Shula Marks. A superb historian of South Africa and great believer in the values of the Commonwealth, she ran the Institute wisely and practically for ten years between 1982 and 1992. She offered me the Chapman Fellowship there for the year 1984-85. It was modestly remunerated but allowed me access to all the university's facilities. In return I offered talks and postgraduate seminars, many of them given not by me but by writers and scholars whom I invited to the Institute. My attachment continued for two years past the period of the fellowship and overlapped with a six-month visiting fellowship I was given at the Australian Studies Centre, housed in the same building. Among the notable Commonwealth writers and scholars who came as my guests to the two Centres in this period were Fleur

Adcock, Mulk Raj Anand, Angus Calder, Nirad C. Chaudhuri, David Dabydeen, Anita Desai, Nissim Ezekiel, Wilson Harris, Christopher Koch, Jack Mapanje, Les Murray, Lauretta Ngcobo, Njabulo Ndebele, Ben Okri, Samuel Selvon, Wally Mongane Serote, C. K. Stead, Randolph Stow, and Ngũgĩ wa Thiong'o. To followers of post-colonial writing this was, as a student said at the time, 'a starry plethora'.

We moved from Milton Keynes Village after only two years of experimenting with modern estate life and finding it wanting. The house to which we moved was in Woburn Sands, a village that had been called Hog Sty End until the railway arrived and Queen Victoria needed to alight at its station to visit the Duke of Bedford at nearby Woburn Abbey. The ancient name was changed so that Her Majesty would not be struck by vulgarity. Today Woburn Sands is almost an extension of Milton Keynes, but it is still surrounded by extensive woodland belonging to the Woburn estate. Dull in architecture, there was one beautiful house, which was the one we bought. It was known by some locals as 'the doll's house' because it looked like one of those drawings which children make. It was square, with an upstairs and downstairs window on either side of a pretty white porch. Its red brickwork was picked out with white edging and the whole building had a vaguely Gothic aspect to it, with pointed window frames. It was called Eden House and for the next quarter of a century it was a kind of paradise for us. We bought it almost by chance. We had been at a 40th birthday party one Saturday night when Helen, for the only time I recall, drank too much. On Sunday morning all she wanted to do was sleep it off and get rid of our daughter and me. She suggested that I take Isabella out, and for something to do look round this pretty house that had just come up for sale a few miles away in Woburn Sands. I fell for it immediately and came rushing back to tell Helen that she must get up to look at the place, the owner having told me that an offer was already under consideration and it would be withdrawn from the market the next day. Grabbing her head, which was still lying on the pillow, Helen struggled down to the car and we drove up to see Eden House together. The rest is history.

Over time and as we could afford it, we enlarged the house. Brian Paver, the architect husband of my Arts Council colleague Jilly Paver, re-designed the back of it, echoing the Gothic hints elsewhere, using old bricks and wood, some of which came from a demolished school in Normandy, but insisting too on modernity. We became well integrated into the local community and loyal members of St. Botolph's Church in Aspley Guise. I was persuaded to tread the boards one last time, portraying Faithful in an adaptation of *The Pilgrim's Progress* by John Bunyan, who had been a local Bedfordshire author. We performed in the commanding church at Husborne Crawley, directed by a retired actress, Jinny Haynes. All went well until the last night, when my father came in his wheelchair to see it. He took it all very seriously until the moment came when I was burned at the stake for my faith. He got the giggles, which until then I had assumed would never bother an octogenarian.

Our children went to Swallowfield Lower School and Fulbrook Middle School, both just down the road, and then to Redborne Upper School in Ampthill. Most of our friends had sent their children to private schools, wringing their hands in *faux* self-exculpation as they did so. Redborne served Isabella well, since she was always likely to feature in the school's league tables of examination success. We felt at times that the unacademic but no less personable Alex was cast adrift by a system imposed by a government obsessed with target fulfilment rather than human development.

Helen went back to the Open University after maternity leave, whilst I busied myself with my freelancing *pot pourri*. I was interviewed for one or two jobs I did not get, including the directorship of Voluntary Service Overseas. My prospects were not enhanced by the fact that I had broken my wrist 'in a hundred places', as the fracture expert told me on the night I did it, and was in plaster and in pain. I had been picking plums from a mouldy tree in our new back garden when a branch gave way and down I went, impacting my wrist on a paved path as I put out my hand to steady myself. Any prospect that I might make my living as a concert pianist was finally dashed. Instead I had a stroke of luck. The founding Secretary of the Open University when Helen first joined it in 1971 was Anastasios Christodoulou, a Greek Cypriot who had moved to the Association of Commonwealth Universities (ACU) in 1980 as its

Secretary General. He lived in Aspley Guise, a mile or two from our house in Woburn Sands. One day, while I was still nursing my damaged arm, he wandered into our front garden to offer us an assortment of vegetables he had grown on his allotment. He asked me if I might be interested in coming to help him with one or two projects, perhaps one day a week. I would not only be receiving some regular payment again, but I would once more be part of a respected organisation. Chris's allotment yielded for me that day far more than a few carrots and courgettes.

One day a week quickly became five. For over two years I was designated the Secretary General's Special Assistant and worked alongside him at the ACU headquarters in John Foster House, Gordon Square, a short walk from Euston Station, to which I now found myself commuting once again. At this time, though it has increased since, the ACU had a membership of over 500 Commonwealth universities and its role was to keep them in touch with each other, to share beneficial development projects and to meet quinquennially. The Association was coming up to its 75th anniversary when I joined. Chris, as Dr. Christodoulou was known, made it clear that he thought most of the staff had probably been there from the beginning. As individuals, they were all extremely amiable to work alongside, but they preferred tried and trusted methods. Chris had presided at the Open University over the establishment of the boldest experiment in British higher education since the war, working with a radical team of young iconoclasts;

at the ACU he found many of his colleagues hard going. He would sometimes ask me along to his office at
the end of the day and over a sherry let off steam. Rather like Derry Jeffares at Leeds when frustrated by the
sedentary traditionalism of some elements in the School
of English, Chris spent as much time as he could travelling the world. He would accept any invitation to anywhere. I recall him going to the 900th anniversary of the
founding of the University of Bologna, amid *sotto voce*
comments among his colleagues that they had not realised Italy was in the Commonwealth.

Helen and I liked Chris and his wife Joan immensely. Both of us felt we owed as much to them personally
as professionally, for they were inordinately hospitable.
Chris asked me to be involved with three projects in
particular for the ACU: updating a published history of
the Association, overseeing a tracer study of former
Commonwealth Scholars and assisting in a major fund-
raising appeal.

The first of these was a steady matter of research. In
Community of Universities (18), Sir Eric Ashby had written what was described as 'An Informal Portrait of the
Association from 1913 to 1963'. My task was to report
on the next two and a half decades and look to the future. A former Secretary-General of the ACU, Sir High
Springer, now Governor-General of Barbados, was the
front man for the enterprise and his name is listed as
main author. I liked him very much and our meetings
when he visited London were always companionable,
but all he really did to the text of what I drafted was

correct my inelegancies of style and write in a few cheerful phrases. Being a ghost writer was a new experience for me, but I am happy with the book we produced, *The Commonwealth of Universities* (19), published by the ACU in 1988.

The tracer study was more complex. We recruited an agency that worked with Government on questionnaire surveys and sent out a series of carefully crafted questions to every former Commonwealth Scholar and Fellow we could trace, in all the countries they came from, asking them about their subsequent careers. It was a huge undertaking. I was given an assistant, Peter Meyer, and together we worked hard at tracking down as many people as possible, but at the time there was no official alumni network and we were conscious that we could only be as effective as the Commonwealth Scholarship contact point in each country allowed us to be. It was especially hard to track down Indian former Scholars. I made a visit to Delhi to try to sort out the difficulty. The office handling the scheme was within the Ministry of Education, a Dickensian trove of piled up documents stretching from wall to wall, all bound in pink ribbon. The clerks were solicitous and tried to help, but they had no more idea than I did about where to search for contact addresses. As a result, there is a lacuna labelled 'India' in the tracer study which hindered what was, in most other respects, a worthwhile exercise in explaining the merits of the scheme.

Chris presented our findings to the next meeting of Commonwealth Ministers of Education, in Nairobi in

1987. We had received an overall response to our questionnaire of 40%, which was regarded as a strong outcome. There were three main findings, some of which were predictable, but no less valuable for having now the evidence to prove them. For example, we provided empirical data showing that women tended to meet a glass ceiling when they tried to re-enter their careers after having children; and there was a shockingly low number of females in senior professional positions in every Commonwealth country taking part. Secondly, a myth was dispelled that Commonwealth Scholars and Fellows tended to stay in their host country rather than return home to help in the development of their nation of origin. This was not true. If someone did stay on indefinitely, they were much more likely to be from a developed country wanting to continue working in a developing country, as once I had contemplated staying on in Ghana rather than returning to Britain. Thirdly, our tracer research had set out to test whether the Commonwealth Scholarship and Fellowship Plan had identified highest quality future contributors to the participating countries, as had been hoped when it was launched in 1959. We found that this was indeed the case, despite the fact that the evidence from such a major country as India was incomplete.

The fund-raising appeal was headed by Thomas Symons, founder president in 1964 of Trent University in Canada. The purpose of the appeal was to raise a million pounds to set up a new fellowship scheme for mid-career academics and administrators from Commonwealth universities. The Queen, who was patron of the ACU, took the unusual step of agreeing also to be the patron of the appeal. Tom Symons helped bring this about through his links with royalty. When he was in London, he would make a point of calling at Buckingham Place or Clarence House. He usually stayed at one of the city's most exclusive hotels, the Stafford. If he invited me to take tea with him there, he would let slip confidentially that this was the Queen Mother's favourite hotel. I could not imagine when the Queen Mum might be staying in any hotel, but it did not matter for the surroundings were charming and scones excellent. Our appeal went well and we raised double our target.

In August 1986 the executive heads of Commonwealth universities met in Penang in Malaysia. I had a number of duties to fulfil and was kept busy, but Helen, our four-year old daughter and our seventeen-month old son were able to come with me. Chris Christodoulou was egalitarian to his fingertips, which may have originated in his childhood when he did menial tasks in the family restaurant in Charlotte Street in central London, a gathering-place for the Greek Cypriot community where everyone was treated as equal. For all the grand positions he held, Chris lacked any sense of hierarchy. He therefore encouraged families to travel to official events with staff members, if they had the resources to do so. The vice-cancellarial spouses at the Penang gathering, which was held at a luxury hotel called the Rasa Sayang, did not altogether share his *camaraderie* and were perhaps understandably out of sympathy with the demands of our toddler, but we did not allow it to spoil our family time together.

We were joined in Malaysia by my brother Colin, who flew over from the Island School in Hong Kong, where he was headmaster. When the ACU gathering ended, Colin flew back to Hong Kong, with us in tow. We loved Hong Kong, a city as much of water and wetlands as it is of high-rise office blocks and corporate companies. We went one weekend *en famille* to Macau, still a Portuguese enclave just as Hong Kong had another eleven years ahead as a British colony. A colleague of Helen's who made the arrangements mischievously chose a hotel which doubled as a brothel, where the numbered prostitutes sat on benches behind a clear glass screen, awaiting customers to pick them out. Only men were allowed in this section of the 'hotel', so Colin and I took a beer and watched the trade unfold. The women looked extremely bored, but every now and then one would respond to an invisible call and leave the bench, reaching for a bar of soap as she did. Helen crept down from our room, pretending to be lost, and took a fleeting view from our side of the glass of that which no woman was intended to see. Our children slept through it all. The next day we took them to the famous Macau casino. Thus were they introduced, if only tangentially, to sex and gambling.

I remained in touch with the ACU until Chris retired in 1996. I was delighted some years later to be asked back to serve initially as a member, and then as the chairman, of the Commonwealth Scholarship Support

Group. This committee liaises with Government, Parliament and the public to promote the interests of the Scholars and to lobby for its financial security. I also kept in touch with Tom Symons and contributed to his 80th birthday celebrations in 2009, which were held in Toronto and were marked by publication of a *festschrift* volume in which I had a chapter on his manifold interactions with the Commonwealth (20). He had been at the meeting in Oxford in 1959 which led to the establishment of the Commonwealth Scholarship and Fellowship scheme and thereafter was a unique force for good in promoting higher education throughout the Commonwealth for the best part of sixty years.

6

COUNCILS: GREAT BRITAIN AND THE
WORLD, 1980s, 1990s and 2000s

In the mid-1980s the Arts Council of Great Britain was under attack for neglecting the interests of black and Asian people. In 1984 it published a famous strategy document, *The Glory of the Garden: The Development of the Arts in England* (21). Bizarrely this took its title from a poem by the writer most identified in the public mind with imperialism, Rudyard Kipling. For the first time an Arts Council report faced up to the transformed cultural diversity of our society. Its response was to set up what it rather stuffily called the Ethnic Minorities Monitoring Committee. I was at the time chairing an advisory panel on literature at the Greater London Arts Association and on the strength of it was invited to join the new Arts Council initiative, which met under the direction of its Deputy Secretary General, the cultivated and benign Anthony Everitt. At the time the Arts Council was administered on rather uncompromisingly rigid art form divisions. Our committee's main proposal was therefore quite radical, because it ran across the whole organisation by proposing that every department should direct 4% of its annual budget to prioritising work derived from African, Caribbean and Asian peoples. I wholeheartedly supported this recommendation, not foreseeing how it would lie in wait to ambush me a year or two later.

As the literature specialist on the monitoring committee I was consulted by the chairman of the main Literature Advisory Panel of the Council, Robert Woof, about the appointment of a new Director of Literature. Robert was a scholar of Romantic poetry and Director of the Wordsworth Trust. He was a brilliant fund-raiser who developed William Wordsworth's Dove Cottage at Grasmere into the internationally known research centre and museum it is today. Robert asked my opinion about the kind of person he should be seeking as the Council's new head of literature to replace the controversial Charles Osborne, who was retiring. I talked up the importance of choosing someone fully committed to the direction the Council was taking regarding minority arts. He then asked who I would think suitable to join the selection panel he was putting together, alongside himself and the Chairman of the Council, the erudite antiquarian bookseller and former editor of *The Times*, Sir William Rees-Mogg. I pointed out the necessity of having a black writer and suggested the poet James Berry. I thought it would also be advisable to have a heavyweight mainstream author and proposed Margaret Drabble. I knew them both and was pleased that my advice was taken. A few weeks later Robert telephoned me again. Interviews had been conducted, but no suitable candidate had been found. He was not sounding me out in any way, but it was obvious that he was floundering as to what he should do next. I reflected for a day or two and then, as much to my surprise as his, decided to apply for the post. I was appointed to it and from that moment to this have advised anyone putting in for a job to see if they can choose their own interview panel. It helps considerably!

Charles Osborne had been Director of Literature from 1971 to 1986. His chief interest in the arts lay in opera, though this did not stop him from not only running the department I was to inherit but also later becoming chief drama critic of the *Daily Telegraph*. He hailed from Australia, was gay, and had a lacerating wit. He emanated charm and bile in equal quantities. He had some fans for what he did for literature at the Council, but they did not include many writers, publishers, editors, literary journalists, scholars, librarians or academics. He delighted in mocking the reputations of many up-and-coming authors and prided himself on being regarded as the foremost Agatha Christie expert in England. Rees-Mogg had come into the Council with a mission to cut the number of organisations dependent on its funding. In this Charles fully acquiesced. Literature had often been described as the Cinderella of the arts; Charles was unkindly described by some as two ugly sisters rolled into one. Following a recommendation in *The Glory of the Garden*, which queried the value of the Council supporting literature at all, he presided over a dramatic cut in its already modest budget. This was so deep that when I took over in 1987 the department's annual allocation was approximately £500,000, or 0.5% of the total available to the Council.

There was an interregnum of a few months between Charles's departure and my arrival, enough time for speculation to build up that the Council would enact the threatened abandonment of literature. Many people therefore greeted my appointment with relief, for it indicated an ongoing commitment to the art. There was a small ripple of interest in the press. *The Daily Telegraph* sent a young journalist along to interview me; his name was Sebastian Faulks. I had until that day, and for a long time after, never had a day off work for illness, but it happened on that particular Monday that I was feeling vile, with a headache, sore throat and ghastly pallor. I should have been in bed. I had come to work because of this impending meeting. I concentrated hard on what I was being asked, but at one point Faulks made a small quip, to which I did not provide the smile of acknowledgement that was apparently sought. The next day his profile of me appeared in his paper, intimating that I had little or no sense of humour and that the Council had made a rather glum appointment after the scintillating Charles Osborne.

I was fortunate that worked I well with Luke Rittner, Secretary General of the Council, and was able to consolidate my friendship with Robert Woof, who shared my ambition to step up the importance of literature. Rees-Mogg was more encouraging than I had feared. My budget might be small, but I was never made to feel that my voice was less equal than that of any other department director. I set about arguing the case for new money and eventually achieved enough to be able to begin some new initiatives, as well as to enhance the annual amount we gave to our regularly funded 'clients', as those in receipt of recurring Arts Council grants were then called.

First, however, I had to contend with a charge of racial discrimination. The 4% shift of funds required across the Council for boosting work from ethnic minorities had been difficult for the Literature section to implement because the whole of its meagre budget was fully committed. The only flexibility lay within the annual Writers' Awards, grants given to assist authors financially as they worked on new projects. In 1987 we only had three such awards available, but it was agreed that our 4% should be invested in these by designating them exclusively for black or Asian writers. Everyone welcomed this, or so we thought. An exception was the poet Fiona Pitt-Kethley. She took the Arts Council to court on the grounds of discrimination against white writers. I inherited the issue and had to gather the case to refute her claim. I was not helped by the fact that the Commission for Racial Equality backed Pitt-Kethley. They had been looking for an opportunity to prove that they did not exist only to represent people of colour. Two public bodies of national standing were now pitched against each other in the courts. On our side we had no problem in securing witnesses to speak up for what the Council had done: James Berry and Margaret Drabble came to the rescue again and were joined by the publisher Margaret Busby. Pitt-Kethley could not provide a single witness to support her. In the end we won the case, with costs awarded against the CRE. Technically we had breached the law, but the tribunal decided that our decision had been fully and responsibly deliberated. Meticulous minutes of meetings leading to the decision proved this. We were in error in not having applied for a certificate of exemption in advance of advertising the awards, but the case established a precedent that, providing such a certificate existed, arts bodies were able legally to discriminate positively in favour of minorities. The Arts Council and the CRE made peace with each other shortly after and the Writers Awards went from strength to strength, with the great novelist Penelope Fitzgerald as an occasional assessor of applications for them. A happy outcome thus followed a situation of stress and uncertainty.

This success encouraged us to venture further into supporting black and Asian professionals through a scheme for them that cost the Council little financially, but which launched several careers. In partnership with both mainstream publishing houses and independent presses, we created placements which provided wide experience of how publishing worked. Up to that point, Margaret Busby had been the *only* senior black person in British publishing.

Within the portfolio of organisations which we regularly funded was the Arvon Foundation. Superbly administered, Arvon had begun in 1968 and swiftly established itself as a much respected provider of residential creative writing courses, first at its original base in Devon and later also at Ted Hughes's former home at Lumb Bank in Yorkshire. After my time at the Council, but with its help, it acquired the playwright John Osborne's former home in Shropshire as a third centre. I have sometimes doubted the efficacy of taught courses in creative writing when offered at universities, though obviously there are some authors so charismatic that it is a privilege to have worked with them in any way, but I never doubted the value of what Arvon offered. Its format brought together sixteen writers in residence for five days, sharing domestic routines such as cooking while at the same time working out the best approach to a poem or story or play or detective fiction or... Over the years the Foundation has explored every kind of genre, but almost always within the tried and trusted formula it devised when it began. David Pease, with the able support of his wife Tina, ran it from 1973 to 2000 with consummate commitment and a unique brand of lugubrious humour.

For four of my ten years at the Council the poet Lawrence Sail chaired Arvon and became a good friend. In an essay entitled 'The Cheshire Cat's Grin' he recalls Ted Hughes conversing with him on the subject of invisibility. It still strikes me as being an excellent analogy of what the Arvon Foundation seeks to do, a metaphor for its unbounded curiosity, adventure, optimism and faith in the creative spirit.

What if, in this age of relentless publicity and promotion, no one had really discovered the foremost writer of the time? Maybe he or she was working away entirely without recognition, perhaps even not having published anything as yet, and to be discovered only subsequently by some perspicacious literary archaeologist. This thesis may do less than justice to human vanity and the desire actually to communicate fully, and may also beg the question of what is meant by 'foremost'; but it remains intriguing nonetheless. As well as pointing to the provisional nature of critical judgements, the notion of the invisible poet seems peculiarly apt in the era of hype. As an image, it has a suggestive strength greater than that of an updated version of the garret-bound ghost of Romanticism. Besides, it is somehow rather appealing to think of a writer being represented, so to speak, entirely by *livres d'absence*. (22)

Hughes's speculation, with its hint of the metaphysical and as remembered by Sail, touches on the mystery of creativity. Can we only define greatness by what we see under our nose or may genius reside in the unknown, rather as Michelangelo believed he was merely the agent for releasing the figure within the marble? Hughes is straying into Gray's country churchyard:

Some mute inglorious Milton here may rest.

Opportunity is everything, but of these unrealised geniuses 'Their lot forebade'. Ted Hughes yearned to let them have their chance. Hence his belief in Arvon, which gave sixteen people a working week to discover themselves and release their art.

I was attending a senior management meeting at the Council one day when a note was handed to Luke Rittner. Would I please go downstairs as the Poet Laureate had called in and would like to beg a few minutes of my time? I could feel my stock rising. I had quickly learned that if one's budget is small, evidence of a good network was not a bad substitute and might in time make it grow. I slipped downstairs to meet Ted and his wife Carol in the foyer. He was embarrassed at having brought me out of a meeting, but there was something urgent he needed to ask about: our funding of Arvon. Ted Hughes has been accused of many personal faults over the years, but I do not forget the genuine humility of his demeanour that day. He need not have worried because at the next feasible moment we enhanced the Foundation's annual grant, making it the largest recipient of public funds for literature in the country.

On 18th March 1993 I went as the Council's representative to a celebration of the life and work of the 'war' poet Wilfred Owen, on what would have been his one hundredth birthday. He had, of course, been killed in the last week of the First World War. Held at the Marches School in Owen's home town, Oswestry in

Shropshire, the event managed to be both a celebration and a wake. The readers were Ted Hughes and the actress Susannah York. Both were excellent, but it is Hughes's rendition of 'Strange Meeting' which I continue to hear down the years. The much anthologised poem tells of two soldiers meeting in the underworld, one having killed the other.

> I am the enemy you killed, my friend.
> I knew you in this dark: for you so frowned
> Yesterday through me as you jabbed and killed.
> I parried; but my hands were loath and cold.
> Let us sleep now... (24)

As Hughes's deep, resonant, Yorkshire accented voice said the lines, there was utter stillness in the school hall. It was as though all the yeomanry of England who had ever died in wars were being remembered. I felt that *frisson* once more, on 13th May 1999 in Westminster Abbey. It was at the close of the Service of Thanksgiving for Ted's life. We had just stood respectfully as the Prince of Wales gently escorted his 98 year old grandmother, the Queen Mother, who had been a fishing friend of Ted's, down the full length of the choir and nave. Then a recording of Ted's voice was heard. He was giving us the threnody from *Cymbeline*:

> Fear no more the heat o' the sun,
> Nor the furious winter's rages;
> Thou thy worldly task has done,
> Home art gone, and ta'en thy wages;

Golden lads and girls all must
As chimney sweepers, come to dust. (25)

The Poetry Society was another recipient of what, in terms of the budget for Literature, was a large subsidy. Unlike Arvon, it seldom seemed out of reach of a crisis. The Society occupied a large house in Earl's Court, full of musty busts of poets like Tennyson. Its cavernous rooms and glum bar shabbily imitated a bachelors' club. My duties required me to sit in as an observer at its quarrelsome board meetings. I was pleased when the Society decided to find smaller, more practical premises and I was with the Director, Chris Green, when they alighted on the building in Covent Garden where they have been ever since. The Society produces an excellent journal, *Poetry Review*, has an ambitious programme of readings, administers the National Poetry Competition, and in countless ways promotes the cause of poetry throughout the country. Today, I am sure, it is a tranquil organisation, but too often in my time it was at odds with itself. There had not been unanimity about its move; nor was there about much else. When my colleagues Gary McKeone and Jane O'Brien produced a research report in 1996, entitled *A Poetry Survey for the Arts Council of England: key findings* (26), the Poetry Society barely featured.

We did, however, financially support various poetry and literary journals. *Agenda*, scrupulously edited by the enigmatic and intense William Cookson, was the most difficult to advise, given the new climate of 'value for money' – code for sales and marketing. No one doubted William's integrity, even his courage. He had been known to send back a poem by Seamus Heaney as not good enough for the journal. He could also show unexpected flair. He told me that he had sent an appeal for funds to Paul Getty. One night sitting in his flat reading some poems, he heard the letter box flap. He went to see what it might be at such a late hour. In a white envelope was a terse handwritten note from the billionaire philanthropist; he had dropped it off himself under cover of dark, accompanying a personal cheque for £10,000. What William lacked was the slightest interest in selling his journal, which had a tiny circulation. He eschewed a re-design of its staid covers, disliked appearing on platforms with his poets, and looked askance at anything to do with figures. It was hard to go on justifying the use of public money in the face of diminishing returns, though when eventually it came to withdrawing an annual grant, there were protests led by the Chairman of the Council himself, Lord Gowrie. My advisory committee held its ground, because it knew it was carrying out the Council's own policy, but it was not an agreeable moment.

More fun were the conversations and occasional lunches I had with Alan Ross, redoubtable editor of *London Magazine*; Karl Miller, Mary-Kay Wilmers and Nicholas Spice of *London Review of Books*; Martin Bax of *Ambit*; Martha Smart who ran the Poetry Book Society, a subscription service for new poetry books; and two inspiring publishers, Peter Jay of Anvil Press and Michael Schmidt of Carcanet. Alan was one of the most respected editors of the last century and I was always slightly in awe of him because there seemed to be no literary eminence whom he had not known. We also shared an interest in India, which led him to commission me to write a piece for the magazine on Mulk Raj Anand. Alan's sudden death in 2001 came only two days after we had been at the theatre together to see Simon Gray's new play *Japes*.

The Council was sometimes criticised for providing a subsidy to *London Review of Books*, which could probably have managed without it. Frankly, however, I thought that we benefited from association with a publication which had quickly staked a claim to pre-eminence not only in Britain but internationally. Karl Miller had founded it in 1979, the year in which industrial action closed down *The Times Literary Supplement*. He was Lord Northcliffe Professor of English at University College, London, and a formidable intellectual. He scared me some of the time, but through my familiarity with uncles in Edinburgh of a similar disposition I soon detected kindness beneath his dour Calvinist manner. He stepped down in 1992 and was succeeded by the American editor, Mary-Kay Wilmers, who with the publisher Nicholas Spice continued to develop the *Review* to its unrivalled position today.

I was also happy to provide Arts Council support to *Wasafiri*, the sole survivor of initiatives taken in my Africa Centre days under the umbrella of the Association for Africa, Asian, Caribbean and Associated Literatures

(ATCAL). ATCAL itself died an early death for want of anyone prepared to take it on after its founders, including me, stepped down. *Wasafiri*, Susheila Nasta editing it with huge *panache*, gradually grew into being the nation's foremost journal of international contemporary writing. I sit on its advisory board to this day.

Peter Jay and Michael Schmidt both had an extraordinary facility for keeping the loyalty of their underpaid poets long after they might have escaped to larger publishing houses. Carol Ann Duffy was a prime example, with her first four collections published by Peter's company, Anvil Press. He had immense charm and infectious enthusiasm. Michael, who founded Carcanet Press, commanded similar admiration among authors. He was not frightened of telling the Council off when he felt we had made a stupid decision, but he also understood the monetary constraints of our budgets and did not ask for the impossible. Combining publishing with his own writing, as well as with teaching and editing, he worked round the clock. In the summer of 1996, I had a long-arranged meeting with him in Manchester. We should have met in his office in the Corn Exchange in the centre of the city, but a few weeks earlier on 15th June the IRA had set off in that vicinity the largest bomb on the British mainland since the Second World War. Michael described his own near miss – he had been late for an appointment that Saturday morning, as had the person he was to meet, so both survived. The police briefly allowed him back into his office to retrieve a few personal effects, but his publishing commitments and records were either destroyed or in-accessible. The Council helped with emergency fund-ing, and Michael carried on Carcanet's business with undimmed determination. Michael and I co-edited an anthology of Commonwealth prose, which joined my anthology of Commonwealth poetry on the Carcanet list. Nearly twenty years after my departure from the Council, Anvil and Carcanet Presses joined forces, which was like a marriage of first cousins.

Book Trust, which existed for the nebulous but vital purpose of promoting reading, was another of our reg-ularly funded organisations. I never missed a board meeting at Book House in Wandsworth. This building had once been Wandsworth Town Hall. It stood at a busy convergence of roads not far from Clapham Sta-tion. Since it housed the national children's library, I could not imagine a worse place for it to be sited. It is a miracle that innumerable tiny tots had avoided being massacred on their way to choose a book. Book Trust had been set up in 1921, but it was Martyn Goff who brought it to prominence. This dapper and gossipy bookseller-turned-administrator ran the Booker Prize from its inception in 1969 to his retirement in 2006. He delighted in *scandales*, but he was also the author of several novels, an antiquarian bookseller, and a world-class conversationalist. We had been having occasional lunches together since long before I joined the Arts Council. There was no doubt that he was pleased by my appointment because he saw it as a way of extracting inside knowledge from what he regarded as the heart of the establishment.

Book Trust's emphasis on children took me into a part of the literary world with which I was only familiar through my own young family's reading. I lost count of how often I read *The Very Hungry Caterpillar* to them or did my Cockney rendition of 'I'll have that!' as Burglar Bill and Burglar Betty eyed up another item to steal. It led me to respond positively to suggestions that we devise a summer school devoted to the promotion of reading among young people. Book Trust assisted, but the project only took off when we encountered Philip Pullman at Westminster College, Oxford, who had been thinking along the same lines. Philip's writing career largely lay ahead of him, but his imagination was already evident in the way he set about designing this school. My colleague Jilly Paver was entrusted with the Council's side of arrangements and we persuaded Penelope Lively, by now a winner of the Booker Prize but also a brilliant writer for children, to open it. It went well and was repeated the next summer.

It is always helpful to take on responsibilities when they may not have been well handled before. I felt from the start that Sir William, Luke, Anthony and all my colleagues were aware that the Council had not served literature well in the Osborne period and were willing me to succeed. I therefore look back on my decade there as a creative time, in which I was given comparative freedom to build up my department's profile through projects we initiated. The children's literature summer school was one. Another was to create a network for placing writers in prisons, where they could encourage inmates creatively. The era of Margaret Thatcher and John Major rarely displayed much sympathy for sentenced criminals serving time, but I had the good fortune to meet Stephen Tumim, H.M. Chief Inspector of Prisons, who was an advocate for making prisoners' lives as humane as possible. One reason for this was to prepare them for rehabilitation in the outside world once they were released. Though the media might often demand that they be locked up and the key thrown away, he believed that no man or woman was beyond redemption. He chaired a committee at the Home Office encouraging the development in prisons of libraries and arts, and invited me to be part of it.

My involvement was revelatory. The Council backed placement of actors, musicians, visual artists and now writers in every category of prison and young offenders' institution. I visited many of them and was always sad as I walked away, thinking that in the approximately six minutes it took me to negotiate my exit with six keys and drive home I was leaving behind people who might not experience this same six minutes for another twenty years. I also sometimes wondered if encouraging inmates to write poems or stories was always as positive as I had to believe it was. A poem about a caged bird or a story about a locked window obviously explored what the author was thinking of his or her own predicament. Were self-understanding and confronting reality always forces for good? I came to believe that they were... I think.

It was clear that illiteracy handicapped many inmates. The chaplain at Bedford Prison, Ralph Willcox, told me that he often agreed to write a letter to a prisoner's mother if in return they would try to read a few paragraphs of a story to him. I saw glimpses of prisoners' frustration. One evening I went with Helen and my children to HMP Bullingdon to see a performance of *West Side Story*, mounted by Pimlico Opera with many of the prisoners. Some inmates were cross about something and banged their cell doors as we passed by. The performance by others, however, was sublime. We wept as, high on a balcony, a male chorus sang

> There's a place for us,
> Somewhere a place for us.
> Peace and quiet and open air
> Wait for us
> Somewhere.
>
> There's a time for us,
> Some day a time for us,
> Time together with time to spare,
> Time to look, time to care,
> Some day!
>
> Somewhere.
> We'll find a new way of living,
> We'll find a way of forgiving
> Somewhere. (27)

In 1998, the year after I left the Council, this residency scheme evolved into an independent Writers in Prison Network. I look back on the work which led to it as ground-breaking and have reacted with horror to attempts by government ministers since then to thwart its vision by restricting inmates' access to prison libraries or to make reading a reward for compliant behaviour. Those who argue along such lines should themselves be placed in cells for 23 hours at a time with nothing to do and no preparation for a future outside.

I knew from the moment I went to the Arts Council that its new determination to foster a multi-cultural approach meant it had to become more outward looking, less parochial or conventionally English. I did not think it should steal the thunder of the British Council, but if, for example, it was to support artistic endeavours in immigrant communities, it needed to develop an internationalist outlook. Black and Asian people had been settling in Britain since Roman times; now there was a new generation of men and women who had either come here themselves or been born here to incomer parents. They identified as British, but still felt linked to the place of their ancestry. There were ways in which their creative contribution could be harnessed and recognised in the literary field: by a major literary festival in the capital city dedicated to its centrality, by touring writers from other countries, by propagating translation. We brought about all three with lasting results.

We worked closely with the South Bank Centre in putting on the biggest celebration of black and Asian literature that had ever taken place in London. This was in 1994 and the title of the event, which spanned a weekend, spoke of its aspiration: *Out of the Margins.* Salman Rushdie had coined the phrase 'the Empire writes back' in an influential article he had written in 1982 (28); we thought of purloining his epithet, but decided instead to place our emphasis on the determination of writers from minority communities to be heard at the centre of British culture, not aggressively striking back but calmly moving in to claim territory which they felt they had a share in by right. They should no longer be perceived as knocking at the door, like servants attracting the attention of the master, but as part of a multitudinous and variegated diversity whose creative excellence was re-defining Britain. It was a thrilling and moving weekend in which many of the best writers in the country participated, there because they refused any longer to be described as marginal.

Bringing published authors to England to read from their work in public was expensive and required an extra staff member, but with colleagues like Jackie Kay, later to be the Makar of Scotland, in this role, the project prospered. Tours were themed: African, Chinese, Guyanese, Lusophone, Indian, New Zealand, Scottish, the last two with Booker Prize winners Keri Hulme and James Kelman participating. Keri spent most of her time in England lamenting the whitebait season she was missing back home. She and Kelman were perhaps in book sale terms the least popular Booker winners ever, but their readings for the Council from *The Bone*

People and *How Late It Was, How Late* were enthrallingly original. When we began the series, we pondered whether there would be audiences for such events. There always were. I knew our idea was successful one wet November night in Northampton when I sat with a large rapt house while the future Nobel Prize winner, José Saramago, read from his work in Portuguese, accompanied by his translator Giovanni Pontiero. Many in the audience came from the local Portuguese community – the Arts Council was reaching out to them as no other national organisation was doing.

I have always believed that Britain suffers from a kind of schizophrenia, its two mindsets perhaps conjoined by avarice. The inventiveness and sense of adventure which built the Empire and created the industrial revolution has always been wrestling with insularity and chauvinism. This is reflected in book purchases, only 3% of which in the 1990s were for translated work. The Arts Council created a fund to support the publication of fiction and poetry written in a language other than English. We had an advisory committee of translators and could call in specialists if a book was proposed from a tongue that none of them spoke. The fund still exists, though it was devolved after my time to English PEN. Not least of its achievements was to speak up for the art of translation. It was not unusual then to find translated works where the translator's name was omitted. Still today plays are often said to be translated by someone who has expertise in stagecraft, but does not speak a word of the play's original language. We also lobbied, with limited success, for the basic payment per word, agreed by most publishers, to be increased.

One day a tall German with grey hair and a penetrating gaze came to see me at the Arts Council. I knew nothing of him and had no idea of what he wanted to talk about. He was with me for over an hour. For the first half of our meeting I listened, but quietly formed the opinion that the man was an obsessive, a kind of mad professor who needed to be indulged until I could politely usher him out. He was indeed a professor, based at the University of East Anglia, but he was far from mad. His name was Max Sebald, or W. G. Sebald, as he is known to readers. He said nothing about his own writing. It was only after he had won the Berlin Prize for Literature in 1994 for *Die Ausgewanderten (The Emigrants)* that I began to be aware of his eminence. His request was for funding for a British Centre for Literary Translation at his university, which he planned to be an international resource. He left my office that morning with a commitment of close to £100,000 to help set it up. I came to love Max very much and was shattered by the news of his death in a car crash in 2001. He would almost certainly have been a recipient by now of the Nobel Prize. I regard my friendship with him as one of the privileges of my life.

My enthusiasm for translation equipped me just a little for a responsibility that came my way in 1989. The European Union had set up the Aristeion Prize for literature; it would be awarded for the first time in 1990, when Glasgow was the European Capital of Culture. I had the task of putting together a judging panel equipped to assess books in every official language of the Union, which fortunately then was only twelve. I invited A. S. Byatt to chair the committee, not because her daughter Antonia was a colleague at the Council but because of her erudition and familiarity with languages. The jury selected the French writer Jean Echenoz as the first winner for his short novel *Lac* (29). I was heartily glad that the administrative responsibility for the Aristeion Prize moved on to Dublin, the next European Capital of Culture, and was not surprised to hear in 1999 that it had been wound up, crushed I suspect by its own complexity.

We invented two literary prizes of our own while I was at the Council. The Raymond Williams Community Publishing Prize was for the best example of local publishing produced annually in England. I had been at Cambridge with Raymond's daughter Merryn, who gave us permission to name the prize in honour of her late father, one of the great radical critics of his generation. The prize money was modest and the attention paid by the national press minimal, but winning the award meant a lot to the small publishing enterprises it recognised. A book such as Debjani Chatterjee's *Barbed Lines* (30), printed in English and Bengali on facing pages, helped considerably to raise the status of minority languages spoken in England.

At the other end of the scale was the British Literature Prize, given for the first time in 1993 and today known as the David Cohen Prize. It arose from a chance remark which Peter Palumbo, who had succeeded Rees-Mogg as Chairman of the Council in 1995, made in an interview he gave to the short-lived newspaper, *The Sunday Correspondent*. He was on confident ground with most of the arts, but when he was lobbed a question about what the Council might be thinking of doing for literature, he did not so much grasp at a straw as build a haystack. 'We are going to run a prize bigger than Booker,' he replied. The next morning the current chairperson of the Literature Advisory Panel, P. D. James, telephoned me at 8.30 a.m.. She was at her most waspish. 'Am I suffering from Alzheimer's?' she asked. I told her this was unlikely as I regarded her as just about the most forensic writer in the country. 'I see we are going to run a prize bigger than Booker. I have no recollection of discussing this.' There was a definite hint of accusation: I was clearly keeping something from her. 'Oh, I'd forget about it. Peter was probably just thinking on his feet. It will go away.'

The next afternoon the 'phone rang again. A quiet voice said 'I hear you are thinking of starting a prize for literature. I might be able to assist'. It was David Cohen. He explained that he was a physician and had access to a family trust which supported the arts. He asked if the Council might value some financial help from this source. With my colleague Perdita Hunt I went to meet David. We left that meeting with the shape of the new prize drawn up, a commitment of funding, and the genesis of a friendship which lasted until David's death in 2019.

Though now named after the man who made it possible, the award was known at its inception, as I've said, as the British Literature Prize. We agreed that it should be for a British writer's achievement over a long period of time. Because this would almost certainly mean that it would go to established writers, it was important to ensure that younger writers or readers must also benefit. We came up with the idea of the winning author nominating a writer under 35, or a literary venture which helped readers under 35, to receive a sum of £10,000 which the Council itself would provide. Later this was to be christened the Clarissa Luard Award in memory of our beloved and radiant colleague who died of cancer when she was only 50.

We did a deal with Coutts, the bank, who came in as sponsors. The judging meetings were held at their headquarters in the Strand, in a board room lined with eighteenth century Chinese wallpaper. In these early years, the award ceremony itself took place in Coutts's splendid atrium. David and his wife Veronica attended every meeting, though they never attempted to influence decision making, coming only out of a transparent love of the arts. Sometimes they were accompanied by one or other of their daughters, Imogen and Olivia, for this was indeed a *family* charitable trust. P. D. James chaired the first jury, followed by Michael Holroyd and later by Andrew Motion. I thought it would be sensible for at least one judge to be from outside Britain: Pierre-Jean Rémy, of the Académie française, agreed to serve and was invaluable. My job, with my assistant Anne

Bendall, was to ensure that everything went smoothly. My worst crisis was when one of the judges, John Mortimer, asked to slip out early from a meeting. I followed ten minutes later to go to the loo and found him in mid panic attack as he could not negotiate the exit from Coutts's labyrinthine premises.

We had agreed from the start that we would flout expectations of a prize like the Booker. Martyn Goff anticipated disaster, predicting that our decisions would result in a lack of momentum and attention. We decided that the prize would be awarded only every second year, to avoid it becoming Buggins' turn. No short list would be announced publicly; that would only serve to humiliate five of the six people on it when they did not win. The choice of winner was made two months in advance of the award ceremony to ensure that he or she could be there. Preserving confidentiality in the intervening period was always a challenge, but it was never breached. We also rode a small storm of protests from people objecting to 'British literature' being defined as work in the English language. The Welsh poet, R. S. Thomas, who had been part of one of our touring programmes, was incensed by exclusion of Welsh. We had predicted this by defining the prize as the British Literature Prize for the English Language. Thomas and others were welcome to set up a prize for British literature in Welsh, Gaelic, Gujerati, or any language written in the British Isles, but they never took up the challenge

V. S. Naipaul was the first winner. For the inaugural prize to go to a writer of Trinidadian and Indian descent said much about the shift in perception and definition we had been helping to bring about. As not long before I had been for two years an associate fellow of the Centre for Caribbean Studies at the University of Warwick, I was able by devious means to discover Naipaul's private 'phone number. I was warned that he would be cross at an unsolicited call, but advised that if I could mention the cash value of the prize he would stay on the line. I duly telephoned, to be greeted by an irate demand, 'Who gave you my number?' I talked over him to forestall him banging down the receiver. 'You have won a prize worth £30,000.' He paused, a long pause; then his tone changed. 'I am so sorry that I was a brisk a moment ago. I have one of my migraines today.' From that moment we were friends. Indeed, we made a short film together to be shown at the award ceremony. Naipaul's speech on accepting the prize was printed the next day in *The Times*. He said that he had moved on from faith in fiction to a conviction that the future of literature lay with biographers. He asked the Society of Authors to nominate a worthy recipient of the Arts Council's £10,000 and thus Rosemary Hill was able to complete her magisterial biography of Augustus Pugin, *God's Architect* (31).

Harold Pinter won the award two years later. As the jury moved closer to this choice, one of their number, Joan Bakewell, took the chairman, Michael Holroyd, to one side. She confessed what I suspect all London's literati already knew: she had had an affair with Pinter over many years. Michael quietly advised her not to be involved in the voting and the moment passed, though not long after we all learned that Pinter's masterly play, *Betrayal*, was based on that relationship. He gave his Arts Council's award to the Citizens' Theatre in Glasgow to encourage new writing for the stage. Its director, Giles Havergal, came down to collect it. I had seen many of his productions when working at Stirling and was delighted to be able to thank him in person for some of the best theatrical experiences of my life.

In 1997 the third recipient was Muriel Spark. I was shortly to meet her in far less comfortable circumstances, but from an Arts Council perspective she was a joy. Muriel told me that she proposed spending the prize on a new Alfa Romeo, she and her companion Penelope Jardine having just driven to London from their home in Italy in a car they obviously thought needed replacing. She decided to give the Council's money to James Gillespie's High School in Edinburgh, the inspiration for *The Prime of Miss Jean Brodie*, so that today's pupils there could benefit from an enhanced library.

To my delight, the prize took off in a big way. Especially in its early years it was well covered in the press and some of the acceptance speeches – Pinter's, for example, which paid tribute to his teachers at Hackney Downs School – have often been quoted. I suspect my involvement with the project may have been why I was invited to be a judge of the Booker Prize in 1994. John Bailey, the chairman, had the grace to ensure that the latest novel by his wife, Iris Murdoch, was not submitted for consideration, unlike another judge, James

Wood, who kept it from us that he was married to a contender, Claire Messud. This was the kind of story Martyn Goff loved, for he would feed it anonymously to the press, then throw up his hands with a disarming smile when asked if he had done just that. '*Moi?* Perish the thought!' James Kelman's novel *How Late It Was, How Late* (32) won the prize, but only after a vote 4 to 1 in favour Jill Paton Walsh's *Knowledge of Angels* (33) had been derailed by Bailey's swithering. One of my colleagues on the jury, Julia Neuberger, rushed from the jury room to denounce our decision to Reuters. My father's sister Mabel, an avid reader, had appealed to me not to choose a book with 'language' in it. I fear I let her down; the word 'fuck' appears on almost every page. I was unperturbed by the fuss because I admire Kelman hugely and was indeed pleased when he joined our Scottish writers' tour not long after. I was glad, however, to have another shot at being a judge of the prize twenty years later – an altogether happier experience.

My years at the Arts Council were full of variety. Sometimes we were in the public eye more than we would wish to be. Our start-up subsidy to a new literary journal, *European Gay Review*, edited by Salvatore Santagati, led to a hostile question being asked in the House of Commons about the possible misuse of public funds. This was still in the era of Clause 28, the iniquitous law disallowing the 'promotion' of homosexuality. On the other hand, a report (34) we commissioned from Violet Hughes on barriers to reading, with contributions from many 'name' authors such as Willy Russell, who had once as much feared going into a public library as a football fan might hold back from entering an opera house, went down well with the press.

'Breaking barriers' could well have been the Council's motto at this time. I was proud of an initiative that brought schoolteachers together for whole weekends, funded by us, to reflect on why they had been drawn to the classroom in the first place. In the company of writers such as Anita Desai they would arrive on a Friday slightly reluctantly, clearly bruised by another week of target-driven form filling. By Sunday afternoon they would leave with a spring in their steps, having, for a moment at least, re-lived the joy of why they had opted for this career in the first place.

What I do not recall with so much pleasure is a sense of crisis management that took hold of the Council in the 1990s. There was endless debate with the Regional Arts Associations, later Boards (RABs), about their relationship with 'the centre' and the extent to which they should be autonomous. A lot of my time was spent contributing to discussion documents, which would then either be adopted or not adopted, only for decisions to be reversed within months. 'Management speak' was creeping into the Council's vocabulary. It was not uncommon to spend time telling a consultancy what one's work was about, only to have it fed back in a set of banal recommendations, accompanied by a huge bill. I sometimes went through these reports inserting the word 'not' before every aspirational *cliché*, as though one would ever aim low or not seek to be creative.

All the arts departments at the Council were advised by specialist panels. After Robert Woof stepped down from ours in 1989, I managed to persuade P. D. James to take on the chairmanship. She was a kindly person who called everyone 'dear' but she possessed, as one would expect from her writing, an acute and practical mind. She once told me that she had learned to be clinical and objective about unpleasant matters, whether a gruesome murder in one of her novels or bad behaviour by a rejected applicant for Council funding, because she had sometimes to clear up blood in the sink when her late husband slit his wrists after returning mentally damaged from the war. The only thing to do was detach herself emotionally. She would often come to the Council building for meetings, but would never take the lift, even if she needed to be on the top floor. She felt claustrophobic in confined spaces. Though getting on in years, she preferred to slog up six flights of stairs. More comfortable therefore were the meetings we had at her home in Holland Park, though one had to negotiate a lot of key unlocking before one was let in. She lived alone and criminals must have been aware of her wealth. Additionally, she did not want her beautiful cat to escape on to the busy road outside.

In 1991 she became a peer and invited me to be her guest at her installation in the House of Lords. I failed to make clear that I had to honour another commitment, which was to speak to some sixth formers in Milton Keynes. This school visit did not go particularly well and I was never sent a thank you letter. Phyllis meanwhile had noticed my absence from the gallery. She said no more about it, but I sensed her disapproval, for she herself was a person of immense courtesy. Just occasionally she belied her amenable, even cuddly persona by an unexpected acerbity. I asked her to sign the petition that circulated among hundreds of authors shortly after the Ayatollah Khomeini's infamous *fatwa* of 14th February 1989 condemning Salman Rushdie and his associates to death for the supposed sin of blasphemy in *The Satanic Verses*. Though as chair of the Arts Council of Great Britain's Literature Advisory Panel she could be seen as the leader of the 'official' literary world, she adamantly declined to add her name, on the grounds that such protest statements were drummed up by accomplices to the media. Forgivingly, I organised a 70th birthday dinner for her in 1990 at the River Café in London. I asked her what dessert she would most like. 'There's only one possibility, isn't there, dear? It has to be death by chocolate cake.'

Shortly after her ennoblement Michael Holroyd took over from Baroness James of Holland Park, as she had become. He probably had more experience of boards and committees than anyone else in the literary world, having negotiated many deals to its lasting advantage. In some ways it was strange that the Council had not come his way before. I enjoyed every moment of working with him. His intelligence, learning, wit, acuity, fastidiousness, good nature and above all humanity were beyond praise. I therefore could not appreciate his dethronement by the Earl of Gowrie, a former Minister of the Arts, when he succeeded Peter Palumbo as Chairman of the Council in 1994. Michael said little publicly about this, but I know he was deeply hurt. Grey Gowrie is a true man of letters, but he misjudged this situation. Resistance to his takeover exploded, led by David Lodge, but sadly Michael departed.

I usually sat in as an observer at meetings of the full board of the Council. It was a privilege to hear members such as Brian Rix and Trevor Nunn deliberate about the current state of the arts in Britain. Senior staff would mix with Council members over lunch beforehand. It was in that way that I became friendly with Sir Colin Wilson, architect of the British Library. Sandy, as he was known, enjoyed talking about books and seemed to single me out for chats. Inevitably I probed about the vicissitudes of the Library itself. He told me that the baleful influence of the Prince of Wales, who condemned the design as more suited to an academy for secret police, had virtually killed his own career. He had not received a single commission since for a major project. As a user of the library, I admire the building hugely, as I believe do most scholars. I was proud to be for several years on the steering group of its Centre for the Book. I look back on Sandy Wilson, who died in 2007, not just with respect but with affection.

My immediate team at the Arts Council was superb. Gary McKeone and Antonia Byatt were two of the brightest and most humane people I have ever worked with. In due course both succeeded me as Director of Literature. I think too of Clarissa, Jackie and Jilly, of Jo

Shapcott, one of the country's major poets, and of those based in the regions such as Jenny Attala in Newcastle, Steve Dearden in Leeds, Kieran Phelan in Winchester and Ingrid Squirrel in Exeter.

I left the Council in 1997, but not before I had assisted Andrew Sinclair in research for his history of the organisation, *Arts and Cultures: The History of the 50 Years of the Arts Council of Great Britain* (35). My main contribution to Andrew's work was to join him for excellent 'working' lunches at the Ivy restaurant. The book was a celebration, but it was also something of a wake, for by the time it was published the Arts Council of Great Britain was no more. In 1994 it had become Arts Council England, with fully devolved Councils in Northern Ireland, Scotland and Wales – though in practice these had existed for many years. Indeed, one of my recurring pleasures was to meet up with my fellow literature directors once a year, rotating between the capital cities, including Dublin. My friendships at that time with Michael Longley and Ciaran Carson in Belfast, Lar Cassidy in the Republic, Walter Cairns in Edinburgh and Meic Stephens and Tony Bianchi in Cardiff, are among my best memories, though sadly all but the great poet Michael Longley are now dead.

*

Family life continued apace. Helen moved back into full-time work at the Open University, eventually ending up as Head of Student Recruitment and Retention, or in effect Academic Registrar, of by far the largest university in the country. It was tough for her. I either did the long daily commute into London from Bletchley or was away on royal progresses round the country visiting projects funded by the Council or the RABs. The children were usually compliant, but they had the normal childhood illnesses, tantrums, need to be transported to ballet classes and football matches, read to at bedtime and looked after when neither of us were around. Looking back on it, I do not think I was a good father in these years. My job often took priority. There was far less talk then about work-life balance, but we knew about the right of women to be as free as men to develop themselves. I would happily go off to work and fund a feminist novel or speak about equality at a conference, while leaving Helen to negotiate almost all of the domestic business of the week on top of her own demanding professional life.

In 1992 we persuaded my parents to move from London to Woburn, believing that they would be better provided for if near to us. Money had been less tight since the death of my grandmother twenty years before. Also, my mother had started her first job when she was over sixty, working as a factotum for a wealthy couple in publishing. It gave her some financial independence. Though she had never set foot outside Britain, she now travelled, staying with Colin in Hong Kong and later in Rome, visiting her youngest sister Rosaleen in Zimbabwe, and accompanying a friend round India. The move to Woburn was, we all felt, in their best interests, she because in her early eighties she was frail and drinking too much, he because his disability made it hard for him to be fully mobile. It worked well for him. The flat to which they moved had a warden who regularly checked on their welfare; we were nearby and ensured that at least once a week a family meal was on offer. For my mother, however, I suspect it was a kind of purgatory. She knew no one, other than us. She was not looking after herself properly.

On the last day of 1992 Helen and I were round at their flat for the New Year observance that no Scottish family can forego, whatever their circumstances. My mother complained of a pain. Perhaps airing my worry about the whole situation, I made a remark which, of all the remarks I have ever made, is the one I most would like to call back. 'Oh Mother, you always complain so much about everything'. It was not only untrue, but, as I said it, she was having a small heart attack. A few days later she went into hospital in Bedford. I drove my father to see her. On the way he asked if I would stop while he bought a pint of milk. As a result, we arrived just too late to have a last rational conversation with her. I walked ahead of my father to her bedside, bent down to kiss her, and she smiled beautifully. What came out of her mouth, however, was gobbledegook, as though she was struggling to speak a Slavic language. I went immediately to find a nurse and told her that I thought my mother had had a stroke. 'Impossible!' she replied. 'I was talking to her just a moment ago and I'm looking for her library book, which she has lost. It's a P. D. James.' Whether she found Phyllis's book, and which one it was, I never found out. Mother did not complete it because she died a few days later. She was 83.

Father stayed on in Woburn until he moved into a care home in 1999. He lasted barely three weeks there before he died. Just as I believe my mother had in some interior part of herself assessed her prospects after her stroke and decided she did not fancy them much, so I think my father, aged 89, clearly tiring and no longer able to look after himself, gazed around his new abode and decided it was not for him. He had kept a diary of public events every day since 1st January 1935. He abandoned it in 1999. He had always been a passionate follower of sport, developing as he grew up a bantering relationship with our son Alex about the merits of Chelsea football club, which he supported, compared to Arsenal, Alex's team. Two nights before he died, I visited him with Alex, who said to him, 'Grandpa, it's Arsenal and Chelsea on Saturday. Who's going to win?' 'I couldn't care less,' my father replied. Alex looked crestfallen and slipped away shortly after, but I recognised a man who was literally closing down.

With the money he left me in his will, we bought a house in Morwenstow, north Cornwall, where we had been for holidays many times. We did not, however, forego foreign travel. Helen participated in a conference of university administrators in Beijing and we went there with Alex, travelling to Xian to see the Terracotta Army and on by train to Shanghai. We all went to New Zealand, where we linked up with my cousin Paddy Mair and his wife Linda. They celebrated New Year by firing off live bullets and Paddy, without benefit of a safety harness, took Alex up a 100 foot gantry on a ship in Tauronga harbour while we looked up aghast. When Helen attended to official business in Auckland, I took the children to visit friends in Sydney.

Africa continued to impinge on my life in various ways. The most glamorous was an invitation to a State Banquet at Buckingham Place in honour of the President of Nigeria. By now we had learned how to behave at such functions, though I disgraced myself by inspecting the underside of the gold plate upon which the main course was served and dropping it sharply with a clang. Princess Anne's husband Tim Laurence was sitting opposite us. 'That'll teach you,' he said. 'Gold retains its heat better than any other metal!'

In 1993 I took on the chairmanship of a small body called the Southern African Book Development Education Trust. It focused on encouraging indigenous publishing in southern Africa, especially in Zimbabwe. We survived for ten years, killed off eventually by Robert Mugabe's intransigent attitude to small press publications. When we first began, the Zimbabwe Book Fair was the biggest in that region of Africa, but eventually the mantle was reluctantly passed on to Cape Town. Mugabe quarrelled with the Book Fair because it insisted on allowing the local gay press to have a stall, even though it only published a book about once every two years. Publishers from outside Zimbabwe pulled out in protest against Mugabe, and though the Book Fair continued it was never the same.

The Noma Award for Publishing in Africa annually recognised the best in the continent's indigenous publishing. I was proud to be one of its trustees for many years. The funding for this was Japanese and it took me on one occasion to Tokyo, where I met the formidable Mrs Noma, who presided over Kodansha, the largest publishing house in Japan. I was received by her in an imposing throne room where she sat in state like Elizabeth I. The award was brilliantly administered in Oxford by Mary Jay, but the judges were mainly from Africa itself. When sponsorship ran out in 2009 after nearly thirty years, it left a giant hole.

I was one of only two European judges who were invited to select Africa's 100 Best Books of the 20th Century, a project conceived by the Kenyan scholar Ali Mazrui and chaired by a former winner of the Noma Award, Njabulo Ndebele. The idea was launched in Harare in 1998 and judged in Accra in 2002, with an award ceremony in Cape Town later that year, attended by President Mandela. It took these four years to read the many books we were assessing.

I was also involved in the 1990s with the Commonwealth Writers Prize, chairing its advisory committee, funded by the Commonwealth Foundation. Every year the award of the prize would move to a different Commonwealth country. In 1995 it took place in Harare. *Captain Correlli's Mandolin* by Louis de Bernières won, a book which had singularly failed to ignite the

Booker Prize jury a few months earlier, despite my advocacy – I loved it, as eventually did several millions of readers. Louis could not be in Harare and so entrusted me with his acceptance speech. I added a few remarks of my own, mainly to the effect that all four novels shortlisted for the award from different parts of the Commonwealth celebrated the diversity of humanity, not least in that there was a homosexual character in each of them. Mugabe's Foreign Minister, Stan Mudenge, was about to hand the prize to me as proxy for Louis. He glared and I was sure he was going to walk out. To his credit he did not until after he had presented the prize, but he did not say goodnight to me.

A few years later the prize was again staged in Africa, this time in Ghana. It was a happier event, with Peter Carey, who had won with his novel *Jack Maggs,* flying in from his home in New York and returning immediately in a round trip of 24 hours that, in addition to the presentation dinner, took in a courtesy visit to the presidential palace. It was my second visit to Ghana since living there and Helen's first.

Salman Rushdie was shortlisted for the Prize in 2000 and decided to make it the occasion for his first visit to India since the *fatwa.* The Indian government had banned *The Satanic Verses,* source of the trouble, so returning now was in the manner of a reconciliation. Salman brought with him his elder son, Zafar, who had not been in India since he was four. I knew Zafar through his mother, Clarissa Luard, my colleague and friend at the Arts Council, who had died the previous year. I was with Salman and Zafar in the function rooms of a Delhi hotel at the moment the international press first set eyes on them. The double doors swung open for us to face a phalanx of flashing cameras. I had never experienced such a dazzling crush; for a bizarre moment I said to myself, now I know what it must be like to be Madonna or Brad Pitt. I also thought back to an occasion a few years before, at Queen Mary College in London when, at the height of the *fatwa*, I had introduced Salman at the launch of his latest collection of stories. Given that we could not announce his appearance in advance, the occasion had been billed as a lecture by me about Rushdie. I genuinely expected a tiny audience. I walked into the lecture room first, breathing a sigh of relief at the fact that it was full. Then came a gasp of stunned amazement, as the fact of Salman's presence sunk in. Whoops of delight ensued. I thanked everyone for their warm personal welcome and then added that I had brought a friend with me, Salman Rushdie. The affection for him overflowed. In Delhi it was much the same. India was glad to have him back. He did not win the prize that evening, which went to J. M. Coetzee, but it hardly seemed to matter.

Like anyone describing himself, however obliquely, as an Africanist, I was caught up in Africa 95, a great celebration of the continent's cultures and creativity. It was the brainchild of Sir Michael Caine, a former Chairman of Booker plc, who had helped establish the Booker Prize for Fiction. He had become a friend through our joint involvement with overseas students, and he lured me into the planning for Africa 95. After his death in 1999, his widow, Baroness Nicholson of Winterbourne, helped establish the Caine Prize for African Writing, which is awarded annually for an outstanding short story written by an African author. Today I am a trustee and chair its advisory council. Michael was one of the most inspiring and kind people I have ever known. He was a shrewd businessman, but at the same time a fervent internationalist. His interests spanned the globe from Russia to Guyana, with his devotion to Africa at the epicentre.

We had met through the United Kingdom Council for Overseas Student Affairs (UKCOSA). This had begun as a lobbying organization aiming to achieve a fairer deal in higher education for the growing number of foreign students coming to Britain to study at undergraduate or postgraduate level. Michael chaired the Council and eventually I succeeded him. During our period of involvement, UKCOSA moved from being a rather student-ish outfit, dedicated but slightly amateur, to being a respected government-funded body whose advice was eagerly sought. Ironically, given how dependent they were later to become on income from international students, the vice-chancellors and principals of British universities were initially opposed to the fee differential between home and overseas students which government introduced in 1984. They felt it was discriminatory and possibly racist.

Under the able direction of Andy Masheter and later Maeve Sherlock, UKCOSA agitated for better conditions for foreign students. There were so many casual insensitivities at the time, some of which may linger today. I recall the case of a student who had arrived at Heathrow and asked his taxi driver to take him to Mottingham, an area of southeast London. Whether deliberately mishearing the foreign accent or not, the driver took him at vast cost to Nottingham. We contacted the cab business at the airport and asked them to be more careful. Students commonly complained that, despite the higher fee they now paid, their courses were not appropriate to their needs. A medical student from Tanzania, for example, told me that everything he studied pertained to diseases normally affecting white people in northern climates, whereas he needed to know about sickle cell anemia and conditions more prevalent in Africa. An Indian student studying agriculture told me the same. Annual harvests where he lived were different from his instructor's, who kept referring to the risk of spring frosts in Suffolk.

Moved by the stories we were told about loneliness and cultural misunderstanding, Helen and I sometimes invited a foreign student to stay with us at Easter or Christmas. There was Ping from Malaysia, who had one leg as a result of a bicycle accident when she was a child. This allowed my mother to say of this person sixty years younger than my one-legged father, 'Ping can get up the stairs quickly. Why can't you?' There was Khalid from Sudan who prayed five times a day and Shuguang, who told of us of horrors in China around the time of the Tiananmen Square massacre which were not known in the west. We enjoyed their visits, though Isabella and Alex found it rather tiresome as they were expected to be on hand to explain why Christmas pudding is set on fire or what makes *Dad's Army* funny.

*

I had worked for the British Council in various freelance ways since the 1970s. In all I estimate that I undertook over thirty tours abroad for it, lecturing on aspects of British and post-colonial writing. I wrote study guides for it on R. K. Narayan and Elechi Amadi as well as a book and an essay on D. H. Lawrence. I devised two poster exhibitions on contemporary British novelists, displayed at Council offices around the world. That had led to a row after Ayatollah Khomeini's *fatwa* demanding Salman Rushdie's assassination. I could not conceive of a survey of modern British fiction that did not acknowledge Rushdie's centrality. *Midnight's Children* had restored a capaciousness perhaps not seen since Dickens and an ebullience of language comparable to Sterne's in *Tristram Shandy*. I appreciated, however, the dismay this aroused within the Council, which had suffered outrages against staff in Pakistan, Norway, and elsewhere, perpetrated by supporters of the *fatwa*. Even I had started to look under my car for suspect objects since the Arts Council, despite lacking P. D. James's support, had been the first public body in the country to condemn the Ayatollah's sentence. Rushdie himself was unhappy at the suggestion that his name should simply be left out of the exhibition. In the end two versions were produced, one with him included and a smaller one for Islamic countries that made no mention of him. I went along with this, but felt dishonourable in doing so.

Not long afterwards I was in Nigeria. I was told that at Ahmadu Bello University in Zaria in the Muslim north of the country I must steer clear of any mention of Rushdie for fear of inciting a riot. I asked for questions at the end of my talk. The first student to pipe up asked 'What do you think of Salman Rushdie and why isn't he in your exhibition?' I breathed deeply and gave a straight reply. To my relief, it was applauded.

In 1997 I was appointed Director of Literature at the British Council. It was the same title as the one I had at the Arts Council. This time, however, instead of replacing someone not generally liked, I followed one of the most admired figures in the literary firmament, Harriet Harvey-Wood. There had been a brief internal placement between us, but most people thought that her *baton* had to all intents and purposes been passed directly to me. Much of my contact with the Council over the years had been instigated by Harriet, and we shared family origins in Edinburgh. Indeed, when on one occasion she invited me to her home for lunch, I met her mother, who when a student had known my professorial grandfather Alexander Mair. Her clear recollections of him were deeply touching. Harriet herself was formidable, the Lady Bracknell of arts administrators, but she had been very kind to me over many years.

My four years at the British Council, 1997 to 2001, seem to me now a postscript to my ten years at the Arts Council. In theory the British Council was seeking new blood. I joined it along with three other directors, all being in what could be described as mid-career. Four years later we all left. I suspect that my three exiting colleagues felt as I did. There were few opportunities to make a difference. After a decade of innovating, it was frustrating to have so little influence. Most of the senior management of the Council was male, had joined it straight from Oxford or Cambridge, and paid lip service to change while not really wanting to be challenged. I recall that at a general staff meeting early on in my time there, for which many directors of the Council's overseas offices had flown in, the matter of a new logo came up. To me the chosen motif, four blobby and unconnected dots on a plain background, was a metaphor for the disjointedness and separation of the constituent units of the Council which I was encountering. I stupidly rose to my feet to say this. I was not frozen out. I was simply ignored.

The British Council had begun in 1934 and was therefore twelve years older than the Arts Council. It operated in 210 countries and had 185 offices. Like the Arts Council, it was theoretically independent of government, but the arm's length was much less evident. If a current government decided to give priority in its foreign policy to Eastern Europe, as it did in the years leading to the fall of the Berlin Wall in 1989, then the Council followed suit. When Nelson Mandela took over in South Africa, the African continent became the theme for a few years. After the attack on the World Trade Center in 2001 focus shifted to the Middle East and to Islamic areas. The Council had two headquarters, in London and Manchester, with much of its business being conducted on trains between these cities. Policy agendas were set in Britain and the country offices overseas enacted them. That at least was the theory. In practice each country office decided on its own priorities, usually according to its own development needs and to its available resources.

People travelled a huge amount in the British Council. It was not unusual to hear somebody say they could not attend an internal meeting the next day because they would be in Brussels. 'What about the following Tuesday?' I would ask. 'I'll be in China.' 'The week after?' 'No, I have to go to Brazil'. I was part of this carousel. There were annual literary seminars, lasting several days, in Germany and Romania. I visited Washington, D.C., though the Council's presence in the United States was quite small on the grounds that the 'special relationship' could be assumed to take care of itself. I visited Johannesburg, where the locally employed deputy director of the Council tried to persuade me that HIV AIDS was a western media plot, racist in intention and belittling to Africa's aspirations. I went to the Calcutta Book Fair, where I found myself addressing an audience of 3,000 immediately following Richard Dawkins, whose chosen subject was 'The Charlatanry of Astrology'. I am surprised we both survived. I took a team of eleven British writers to Hong Kong shortly after the handover. We were warned that the local people did not read books and would not be interested. We found the opposite to be true: every event was sold out. I recall one of the team, Andrea Levy, telling me how much the whole experience had meant to her personally. It would be a mistake, she said, to think that the value went only one way. John Agard, Bernardine Evaristo and Grace Nichols were also part of this tour, for we were determined to show that Britain had become a truly diverse nation.

An experience of eight years earlier affected me throughout my time as a director at the Council. It was Saturday 26th April 1989; I was in Poznan, Poland, with the poet James Berry. We were there to talk about new British writing with thirty Polish teachers of English. 'One us is a spy,' the first contributor told us at the opening of the gathering. 'It might be me or this person next to me. You will never know, so just carry on and say what you like'. It was the period when the liberal movement, Solidarity, was flexing its people power and state intimidation was waning. After the introductions, in which James and I formed an impression that the teachers had read every bit as much modern writing as we had, we took a short break to stretch our legs. We walked round the pretty lake in the grounds of the conference centre. It was lightly drizzling. We returned to our meeting room and were told that the BBC World Service was reporting a devastating explosion at a nuclear power station over the border in Ukraine at a place called Chernobyl. The official Polish media, still under Communist control, said nothing. Indeed, the top item on its English language radio service celebrated the official visit to Warsaw that day of the President of Cyprus, which may have mattered to some Poles, but I suspected to be of less immediate concern than the radioactive cloud passing over their country and said to be dispersed to those on the ground by rain. I was taken to one side and told I should not worry: the danger level if one is exposed to radiation is 500 isotopes over the normal, and we were only 50 over. Two hours later an official spoke to me again, ashen faced: the level of radiation over our part of Poland was not 50 over the norm, but 5,000. I am a dead man, I thought. I went to Warsaw the next day to stay by arrangement with Dick Alford, the Director there and a friend since our school days together. His family had been evacuated back to London the day before, Dick dutifully remaining in post. We went the Teatr Powszechny for the first night of a play in Polish about the execution of Mary, Queen of Scots. I knew how she felt. On return to London James and I were both tested for radiation and registered negative, but the doctor blithely said that the test was not infallible, so we could not know for sure.

I thought about this incident every time I travelled thereafter on Council business. In any situation there is risk of the unexpected and dangerous. In Poznan, however, there was the complication of obfuscation. The state authorities were not telling the truth; the Council was kept in the dark, but we had to keep the flag flying.

We were onlookers peering into another culture, trying to make sense of it, but always outsiders. It mattered less, perhaps, in a benign country like France, where we put on a major conference on biography with Michael Holroyd and Zadie Smith participating. It mattered a lot if one was in Russia or Myanmar.

I took a group of Scottish writers to Moscow. After they had given their excellent readings, we would go to a restaurant or a jazz club with our Russian partners. Under cover of the music, piped or live, we would talk about repression, the absence of democracy and the ability of the KGB to re-invent itself. Furtive conversations, they had the effect of making me question how useful our visit really was. My doubts were in the end dispelled by a chat I had with a teacher who had travelled all the way to Moscow from Tashkent, paid for by the Council. She told me of the constraints under which she lived and worked. To her the Council's support was a breath of fresh air; it gave her hope and purpose. I returned to England feeling it was all worthwhile.

In Myanmar I stayed with the local Director, Claus Henning, and his wife. They quarrelled all the time and used me as a conduit for their recriminations. Claus arranged for me to give a lecture on contemporary British writing in the newly refurbished Strand Hotel. I was told it was the first public lecture given by a British person in the capital city since 1948. Most of Rangoon, now Yangon, was very run down, but the hotel had smart conference facilities; in these I addressed a packed audience. It fell into three categories: eager students, venerable elderly scions of the Raj wearing club ties and blazers, and black suited Tonton Macoute look-alikes with dark glasses fringing the walls of the lecture room. The next day we went into the Council's office. I understood then how much of a lifeline the organisation could be for people living under despotic regimes. The ground floor was heaving with young men and women watching BBC bulletins on a television monitor. Some of them were sitting on the top of filing cabinets, others were squeezed into cupboard openings.

I escaped the Hennings's embrace just once, when they loaned me their driver so that I could locate the house where my father had spent the first seven years of his life. To my amazement the street was still called Windemere Drive and easily found. The house was intact, though now lived in by an army officer with high security, which prevented me going beyond the gates. Back home I told Father about the house. He wanted to know if it retained the tennis court down a slope to its left side, which is where he had first played sport. I was able to tell him that it did. It was like the completion of a circle, for he died three weeks later.

Cultural misunderstandings, perhaps better described as insensitivities, cropped up from time to time in unanticipated ways. Much the most serious affecting my work occurred in Germany. Alan Hollinghurst, Glyn Maxwell, Caryl Phillips and Graham Swift, four front-ranking authors, were touring for the Council. At supper in a restaurant in Frankfurt, hosted by the local Director, they awaited their meal. Caz Philips casually sampled a bowl of peanuts. Mrs British Council smiled sweetly and said to him, 'I see you are going back to your roots!' A chill descended. Caz is black; the other writers were white. Graham spoke quietly to the lady, 'You realise what you have just said?' He was giving her an opportunity to escape, but she repeated her comment. All four writers walked out.

I received a telegram about this incident while I was in Malaysia. It was close to Christmas. I arranged to meet Caz on Boxing Day in the foyer of the Royal Festival Hall. It all came tumbling out. It was not just this incident. There had been many over the years, not only aimed at him but almost endemic in how non-white people working in any capacity for the Council had been treated. It was time to end it once and for all. The four writers who were in Germany had already called on their fellow authors to boycott the Council. Salman Rushdie among others had signed a protest. Over three hours, Caz and I agreed on a twelfth hour strategy.

To cut a long story short, the matter was placed before the Chair of the Council, Baroness (Helena) Kennedy. She took it extremely seriously and imposed a policy on all Council staff, wherever in the world they worked, at whatever level, of mandatory race awareness training. She saved the day and our Literature work was able to go on, but it had been a close-run thing. I was shocked, and remain so, at the stories of casual racism within the Council that Caz revealed that day. By the action she took, Helena Kennedy may have rescued from oblivion the organisation she chaired.

For years the Council had administered a summer seminar of two weeks' duration at Downing College, Cambridge. It was efficiently led by Christopher Bigsby and Damian Grant. There were fifty participants, each nominated by the Council in their country of origin, so in a typical year there would be fifty nationalities present, ranging from Azerbaijani to Zimbabwean. Attendees could come from any background, providing they were committed to finding out more about modern British writing: teachers, academics, publishers, editors, librarians, journalists were there. Talks and readings were given through the fortnight by some of the best authors in the United Kingdom. A few, like Doris Lessing, were regulars. I admired how Harriet had built it up, but I was not prepared for the cool reaction I received to adjustments I proposed. The almost total absence of black or Asian writers was one limitation; emphasis on the well-established at the expense of the up-and-coming was another. I also saw potential in adding playwrights to the programme. I loved every moment of these weeks of the five Cambridge Seminars I put together, but I was never fully freed from a feeling that I was a poacher on someone else's estate.

One of the 'stars' who always came to speak at the Seminar was the critic George Steiner. His traditional slot was as final speaker. In my second year he said that he would not be able to speak at 11 a.m., but must because of another commitment come at 9 a.m. I saw no problem in this and invited Jackie Kay to take the later time. Chris and Damian expressed doubts. Who was this Jackie Kay? Did I not understand that Steiner was a great man and it would be humiliating if the Seminar ended with a dud? Steiner duly came and, as always, spun his linguistic elaborations with masterly erudition. Jackie, a performance poet and storyteller whose warmth and wit are almost unrivalled, then gave one of the best sessions I have ever heard at any gathering. The doubters were momentarily silenced. The Seminar grew more diverse after that and I could start to design it as I believed best represented modern Britain.

This did not mean that only younger writers or those from ethnic minority backgrounds were added to the invitation list. For example, I persuaded Harold Pinter to come along and talk about his work. I had come to know him through my membership of English PEN, of which he was an active supporter. He gave an absorbing account of what drove him as a writer, but I felt for the Moroccan participant who dared to arrive five minutes after Harold had begun his talk. He was told that interruptions of this sort were unacceptable because they destroyed momentum and coherence.

Muriel Spark had never spoken at a Cambridge Seminar, but agreed to do so after my dealings with her at the Arts Council over the David Cohen Prize. She was easy to deal with over the arrangements and in top form when she spoke. Almost as though in a parallel universe, however, she was at war with the Council over a book we had commissioned in our 'Writers and Their Work' series. These excellent critical monographs were edited by Isobel Armstrong; unbeknown to her, the person invited to write a study of Muriel's work, Bryan Cheyette, was anathema to the author. According to Muriel, he had in another publication given a false account of her ruptured relationship with her son, the elements of Judaism in her upbringing and her conversion from Judaism to Roman Catholicism.

On a day when my daughter was sitting at home in Woburn Sands, revising for her 'A' level by listening to Geraldine McEwan's recorded reading of one of her set texts, *The Prime of Miss Jean Brodie*, the telephone rang. A Scottish lilt at the other end asked Isabella if her father was in. Isabella said that I was out. 'That's a pity,' came the response, 'because I may have to sue him for heavy damages, and if I don't get satisfaction I may have to take my case to the European Court of Human Rights.' The serendipity of the two voices, Muriel's on the 'phone and Jean Brodie's on tape, did not faze Isabella, but it may have helped her on her way to a good exam result. That was the beginning of a saga that ended with both Muriel and Bryan far from happy, though his book did eventually come out (36) and the Council was not sued. At one point I consulted the Society of Authors as to how I should proceed, since it partly exists to advise writers on their legal entitlements. Mark Le Fanu, its patient and courteous general secretary, let out a slow sigh, an expression half-way between exasperation and experience, as he told me that the Society's Muriel Spark litigation file was approximately ten times bigger than any other writer's.

There were good aspects to my years at the British Council. I was re-united with my old colleague from the Arts Council, Jonathan Barker, who became my deputy. My work had a greater focus on the teaching of literature and the English language than it had in my previous role. It also embraced a rather nebulous concept of 'British Studies', about which I was never fully convinced but which at least had the merit of bringing me into contact with the sparkling social commentator and singer Billy Bragg.

I was also able to re-fashion the Council's advisory committee on literature, though it was never to be as innovative as its equivalent in the Arts Council. The novelist Michèle Roberts agreed to chair it. She and I went together to Egypt where we gave talks in Cairo and Alexandria. At the Women's University we spoke to 300 young women, all of whom were veiled; the staff, however, wore western dress and lipstick. I asked if the young women were attired thus because their fathers would otherwise prevent them from having a university education. My speculation was quite wrong. They chose to present themselves in this way as a form of national and cultural self-expression. I realised how easy it is for outsiders to impose stereotypes on another group that they neither know nor understand.

At the time I worked for the British Council, everyone retired on their sixtieth birthday. I could see that looming, though it was still a few years off. Maybe as an encouragement, I was awarded the O.B.E. at New Year 2000. For my investiture at Buckingham Palace a few months later Helen, Isabella and Alexander were by chance seated in the front row, thus able to overhear some of Her Majesty's conversations with other recipients. Mercifully, they did not listen in to the chat I had with the person behind me in the anteroom. His name was Alan Shearer and I asked him what he did. 'Something in football,' he replied. 'Oh God!' said Alex, as he saw me come across to be invested, followed by Shearer, 'Dad won't know he plays for England.' Indeed, I did not, but I was soon put right by all of my family as we milled around after the ceremony.

I could not see myself retiring as early as 60 and so began to look round for other openings. In truth, I felt that I was treading water. Real decision making lay in the countries where the Council worked, rarely in London, but when a major policy change was signalled from the Centre there was no way of embracing the views of any but a small group at the top. For me, a last straw was closure of most of the Council's libraries overseas, though mercifully India was exempted. To wind up libraries in book-starved Africa was crass. There seemed to be a suspicion of books in many parts of the Council. In Singapore I asked if they still stocked classic authors on their shelves; I was told that indeed they did and taken to see a video collection comprising the BBC version of *Pride and Prejudice* and other Sunday evening television series. In Tokyo a collection of 40,000 books had been given away and replaced by computers; the place was empty when I visited shortly after, as every educated Japanese home of course had a computer. Meanwhile membership of the Council in the country had dropped by approximately 40,000. Back in London I asked if I could discuss library closures with the top brass at the Council. Books are the tools of the trade for anyone working in literature and education. I believed that to dismantle collections all over the world without discussing it with me as Director of Literature was not only discourteous but made no use of my experience. After many weeks, a meeting was arranged with some of the Council's officers. It was timed for 4.45 p.m. on a Friday. The chairman began by saying that he would have to leave by 5. I understood then that the meeting was simply to placate me.

I decided over the weekend that I must leave the Council. On the Monday morning I received an unsolicited call from Cumberland Lodge. Might I be interested in applying for the post of Principal?

7

LODGE AND ONWARDS: WINDSOR AND LONDON, 2001 to ?

I applied and was appointed. The post I took up brought together all my interests in one place. I could not believe my luck. Since it was a residential position, it meant living in a beautiful landscape, Windsor Great Park. We were instantly welcomed by the Park community and played a full part in its life for the next twelve years, aided by the arrival in our family of a bounding black Labrador, called Ben, who needed exercise whatever the weather. Because of Ben we endlessly explored the woods, ponds and grassy areas of our surroundings. Some were laid out formally as gardens or polo pitches, welcoming to the public, and others were left to nature.

Cumberland Lodge exists to bring together people of all generations, but especially young people, for discussion and enquiry. Helen and I soon felt that we had our own private university in our back garden. I was left free to determine the direction the foundation took, providing I reported to the board of trustees. Over more than fifty years ethical, moral and social issues had dominated its agenda. I saw no reason to change that, but I brought to the programming perhaps more emphasis on cultural connections and international matters. The key to it all was hospitality. Meeting and greeting our guests, whatever their background, became a way of life. I loved every minute of it. Not a day passed at the Lodge that I did not give thanks for the sheer fun of the place.

The Lodge dates from 1652 when, after the execution of Charles I, Oliver Cromwell sold crown lands to raise money for paying his army. This is not the place to rehearse its long history, so much of tied to national affairs. Shortly before I left, however, I wrote *Cumberland Lodge: A Brief History and Guide* (37), in which I summarised information I must have imparted a thousand times when showing visitors round. Here early in Queen Anne's reign Sarah Churchill, Duchess of Marlborough, had virtually conducted the affairs of England, with the Secretary at War, Henry Bolingbroke, often in residence. Sarah's husband, the victor of Blenheim, died here in 1722. William Augustus, Duke of Cumberland, lived here as a spoil of war for winning the Battle of Culloden and saving his father's skin. To commemorate him after his death, the house was re-named Cumberland Lodge. I found it hard, as a Scot, to acknowledge that the place at which I worked memorialised the Butcher of so many Jacobites.

Queen Victoria's daughter, Princess Helena, resided at Cumberland Lodge for a long period, re-modelling it after a devastating fire in 1869. One of her regular guests, Benjamin Disraeli, described it as the coldest house in England with the worst food. Neither was true now. I rarely received complaints from people staying at the Lodge, but if I did it was usually a small grumble about it being too warm. As for the cuisine prepared by Robert Szewczyk and his team, it always scored top marks. We modernised the kitchens while I was there, winning an award for the best refurbished kitchen in Britain. We also overhauled the dining rooms, though I insisted that we leave in place a heraldic device associated with Guy Fawkes, as well as memorabilia from 1936 when Prime Minister Stanley Baldwin spent three days with Edward VIII's private secretary, Alec Hardinge, to resolve the crisis over the King's determination to marry Wallis Simpson. It was from the Lodge that the King was advised that he could keep the throne or marry Wallis, but not both.

Some of the drama of the Abdication was re-created in the film *The King's Speech*, which was partly made at Cumberland Lodge in 2010. That came about through a connection I had with Meredith Hooper, mother of the film director, Tom Hooper, who first came to the Lodge for a surprise party on her birthday. Filming took place as a large group of German students were in residence. More than once we had to ask the film's star, Colin Firth, to placate ruffled feathers as the film crew sealed off areas of the building from our academic guests.

The house oozed history but I never tired of pointing out that for all its royal connections it was a republican building in origin, with impeccably radical credentials.

The Lodge's modern story begins in 1947, when George VI made it available for its present usage. He and his Queen Elizabeth had been impressed by a book published in 1943 called *Darkness Over Germany*, written by an academic historian called Amy Buller. Buller had led two higher education deputations to Germany in 1935-6, attempting to understand what was happening to the universities there under Hitler's authoritarian rule. She recorded conversations with students, academics, soldiers, priests and others, many of them examining the philosophical and religious premises upon which Nazism claimed to be founded. The book is a fascinating first-hand account of what was going on in Germany at the time, a country the author knew well and particularly admired for its culture, in so many ways akin to Britain's. Buller has sympathy for the young people of Germany, unanchored by any solid beliefs after the humiliations that had befallen their parents' defeated generation and attracted to the 'high-sounding intellectual phrases' of Nazi populism.

Towards the end of her book Buller describes an encounter in Nuremberg in 1935 with young foreigners from many parts of the world who had come to attend a Nazi party congress. She could perceive that the alienation they felt could easily be transposed to British youth, should our economy turn sour and our drift towards materialism go unchecked.

In the world from which they came there may not have been the desolation that was in Germany, but in their countries too many of the young men were uncertain about jobs and even less sure of any fundamental standards, moral or spiritual. Their right to feel any real part in the life of their country was, if not challenged, often ignored, and certainly this demand that they should prepare themselves for an important role must have been difficult to resist. Unaware of the dark sides of Nazi teaching and practice they were justified in being impressed with the health and happiness and apparent freedom of the young Germans among whom they camped. (38)

Amy Buller wanted to deter young people from the lure of extremism, a mission as relevant now as it was in her day. She discussed with the King and Queen, as well as some highly placed churchmen, the idea of a residential discussion centre where students could reflect on the contributions they hoped to make to society when they graduated. Cumberland Lodge, as we know it today, came out of these conversations.

Shortly before I applied to be Principal, I had participated in a conference there on the arts, in the company of Alan Bennett, Melvyn Bragg, Peter Hall and other luminaries. I could see that it was a place of influence, encouraging relaxed and personal interchanges in the bar as much as pronouncements from a platform. I was interviewed first in London by Eric Anderson at the Heritage Lottery Fund, which he chaired. He was also chairman of Cumberland Lodge. A fuller interview followed at the Lodge itself, where to my consternation I found myself facing seventeen trustees. To my delight, they approved of me.

I knew that matters had not worked out with the previous Principal, who had come from being headmaster of a minor public school. He had been asked to leave and an interregnum of over a year followed, with two temporary heads. The second of these was Norman Gower, who had been a colleague of Helen's at the Open University. He gave me helpful briefing notes in which he pulled no punches about the deficiencies as well as strengths of the place. We moved into Groom's House, a handsome Queen Anne residence that went with the post, though as Helen continued in her senior role at the OU, we coxed and boxed between Windsor and Woburn Sands for the six years until she 'retired', which she did partly to spend more time supporting me. When at the end of our time at the Lodge we were both offered Life Fellowships, I was deeply moved on her behalf, because it recognised the value of her unstinting help and quiet common sense, which many members of the staff had come to appreciate.

I often reflect on the advantage of succeeding someone in a job who has not been successful or popular. It had happened to me at the Arts Council and now it happened again. The governing body is desperate for a similar situation not to arise. Unless one proves hopeless, there is only one direction of travel: up. Everyone was willing me to succeed, partly because they felt a *malaise* had befallen the Lodge. It could look back on a vibrant programme of activities since opening its doors in 1947, but it was slightly resting on its laurels. A glorious past spoke for itself: old visitors' books recorded the participation of great intellectuals in weekend retreats of the 1950s and '60s – T. S. Eliot, Iris Murdoch, Karl Popper. Lord Denning, perhaps the most famous of twentieth-century judges, had chaired the board for years. Margaret Thatcher had come when she was a student, Margaret Roberts, and I was told that when the floral ceiling decoration in the Tapestry Hall at the entrance to the Lodge had been re-painted in the 1980s under a youth employment scheme she had come to inspect their handiwork and added her own splodge of paint to one of the roses. As I guided guests around, I would always ask them to identify which rose it might have been: 'the one with the most frugal use of paint,' I would say, to wan smiles all round.

Alas, one cannot feed off history alone. The foundation was barely surviving financially, saved only by a grace and favour arrangement with the Crown. The Queen herself had signed, as her father had before her, a document entrusting the Foundation with care and upkeep of the Lodge and its surroundings, provided we used them for educational purposes. In 1982 a predecessor as Principal, John Vaizey, had enlarged use of the Lodge to include groups paying higher rates, which could then be used to subsidise student visits and help with the maintenance costs. These 'senior' groups, as we called them, had more ambitious dining menus than the students. It was stipulated, however, that all such groups must be in tune with the mission of the Lodge – no tobacco companies, no shareholder meetings, no nightclub activities. The formula worked well, but it relied on good occupancy of the Lodge's facilities. By 2001 this was no longer the case.

A problem was the human capacity to handle only so much business. I set about attracting new groups, but after a few months, as business increased, a deputation of kitchen and household staff came to see me. I was at risk of abusing their good will by over-stretching their resources. They wanted me to indicate better what I was planning, since it affected all of them. I remembered a similar *cri de coeur* from the staff in my early days at the Africa Centre. Both visitations were wake-up calls. They taught me that I could only carry the staff with me if I always explained to them what was happening and sought their views. Gradually, with their support, we secured a stronger business base. By the time I left the Lodge in 2013, income to the Lodge had tripled and I had a superb team in place.

I sometimes felt that Cumberland Lodge operated in two time zones. On the one hand it was an historically listed country house, elegantly furnished with items on loan from the Royal Collection. On the wall of the bar hung a copy of the census return of those who were living and working there during the era of Princess Helena. Everyone recorded thereon, from the princess and her husband to the under tweenies and gardeners, must have felt then, as we felt now, that they were privileged guardians of the Lodge. We were all passers-through and eventually passers-on.

My Domestic Bursar, Jane Whaley, had joined as a kitchen help in the 1980s. Her housekeeping standards recalled another age. She had the sharpest eye for an unpolished door panel or a dusty chandelier, and an unsurpassed skill in redeploying worn fabrics and finding bargain wallpapers in sales. She arranged house and garden parties better than anyone I have ever known. No sooner was the Christmas revelry over than she was planning a summer fête. She worked seamlessly with Sharon Alloway, who was born and brought up in the Great Park. Sharon, in charge of the dining rooms, never forgot a face and therefore was the person to whom I first went if I needed inside information either about the locale or a guest. Together they embodied a vanishing quality of service. We were lucky too to have had for thirty years or so one of the best chefs in Britain, Robert Szewczyk, who was not only a superb cook but a brilliant trainer of his team. The food was always superb, whether it was to line student stomachs with ballast or to woo the highest paying groups.

The Lodge hosted and provided some of the most progressive discussions anywhere in the country. To avoid these becoming jaded and uninventive, which had threatened when I took up my post, I recruited some eager new staff. They included young fellows, appointed on a visiting basis. I sought the Queen Mother's permission, which she readily gave, to call these the King George VI and Queen Elizabeth Fellowships. We were, after all, officially registered with the Charity Commission as the King George VI and Queen Elizabeth Foundation of St. Catharine's, St. Catharine being the patron saint of discourse. The first fellow was Alois Mlambo, a Zimbabwean historian living in exile, who later became Professor of History at the University of Pretoria. We thus put out a signal that diversity would be part of the Lodge's agenda. Later fellows included Stephen Fletcher from Grenada and Dan Washburn from the United States.

Sometimes circumstances allowed us to extend the appointment of a particularly able fellow. Faye Taylor, who moved later to be in charge of international policy at the Department for Education, was one such, and Owen Gower, now Director of the UK Council for Graduate Education, another. Owen stayed ten years. Shortly before I left the Lodge, he became head of its programme. His intelligence and exemplary public communication skills were matched by great personal kindness and courtesy. I also appreciated the *brio* and networking skills of Ginny Felton, who was initially brought in to manage the Commonwealth Writers Prize when this was devolved to the Lodge by the Commonwealth Foundation for a three-year period.

Martin Newlan came in my second year, doubling up as my deputy and bringing with him a wealth of valuable business experience. He was never afraid to roll up his sleeves to oversee a practical task, but he also had a responsible attitude to the Lodge's finances. His predecessor had become rather gung-ho about expenditure. Martin supervised a huge programme of physical upgradings. New window frames, doors that met health and safety standards, the kitchen refurbishment, changes to the lay-out of the grounds to return to their original design, the introduction of Wi-Fi in every room – these and many more improvements allowed the Lodge to maintain its reputation as one of the best conference retreats in the country, with appropriate accreditations. I mastered the art of being an appreciative onlooker and then garnering the praise.

My personal assistant Jennifer Streek had already served three Principals. With the help of our fundraiser Christopher Mann, who had been working in the Lodge's interests for over forty years, she administered our annual financial appeal. It was always a challenge to raise funds for Cumberland Lodge, because of its Crown patronage and its handsome appearance. That we were able to do so, bringing in significant sums over and above our earned income, enhanced our charitable mission and extended our reach.

I was also fortunate to work with the perhaps the best governing board I ever experienced. Eric Anderson, who was made a Knight of the Thistle in 2002 alongside my former Stirling University colleague and Dunblane neighbour, Stewart Sutherland, was loved by the staff, as was his wife Poppy. I had briefly met Eric in 1970 at Fettes College in Edinburgh, where my brother Colin was teaching, and we were both currently on the board of the Millennium Library Trust. Eric was now Provost of Eton College, where he had once been headmaster. As Eton was nearby, Eric and Poppy took walks in the Great Park and often dropped in to say hello to whoever was around at the Lodge. Eric was a reticent man, for all that he had taught three princes of the realm, three Prime Ministers, several notable actors, and a panoply of public figures. We knew that he had the ear of the Royal Family and had been privy to the Queen Mother's reminiscences, though these were not to be published for fifty years. He had a droll sense of humour, but as the son of kiltmakers in Edinburgh he had a keen business eye and an instinct for whatever would bring advantage to Eton or to Cumberland Lodge. He encouraged me to expand the Lodge's remit and seemed to approve of what I did. He also asked Helen, after she had retired from her university position, to take on the administration of a small charity, the Manifold Trust. He and Poppy used the Lodge one year for a family Christmas. I assured them there would be no problems. Within an hour of me saying this and leaving them on their own to mind the Lodge there was a fire alarm and the boilers failed.

Sometimes Eric would ask me to meet him at his home within Eton College. At the bottom of the entrance staircase was a portrait of Jacob Rees-Mogg, son of my former boss at the Arts Council. His aura had been passed on to a young man opposite whom I sat one day when Eric asked me to stay for lunch. This young fogey type was studying for his 'A' levels. 'What are you hoping to do next?' I enquired. 'I shall be going to The University,' he replied. He clearly meant Oxford.

'Oh, you are going to Luton, are you?' I responded. He was not amused. I was awestruck by Eton's facilities, especially its library, containing so many treasures. I chaired a talk in Windsor one day by Andrew Adonis, who at the time was Under-Secretary of State for Schools. He said his ambition was that every school in the country should be 'like the one down the road'. He gestured vaguely in the direction of Eton College. Dream on. Had he seen their priceless heritage and could he really mean what he was saying?

Our treasurer for much of the time I ran the Lodge was John Pool, who had held many senior positions in City businesses. He was involved with the Lodge for more than twenty years. He and his wife, another Poppy, were great supporters. So were all the trustees with whom I worked, among them Eric's successor as Provost of Eton, Lord Waldegrave; two former Permanent Secretaries, Sir John Gieve and Sir David Hancock; the novelists Susan Hill and Salley Vickers; a prominent civil engineer, Joanna Kennedy; the first police Chief Constable to be given a damehood, Elizabeth Neville; the ever articulate Chief Medical Officer of England, Dame Sally Davies; the retired Dean of Westminster, Michael Mayne; and James Stewart, who later presided over global infrastructure at KPMG. Baroness Prashar of Runnymede and Lynne Berry had both held several chief executive roles in the charitable sector.

In 2010 Eric stepped down as Chairman of the trustees. At my suggestion Sir Stephen Wall was invited to replace him. Stephen had been British Permanent Representative to the European Union and had also spent part of his career within 10 Downing Street. I first met him through David Hancock. Like both David and Eric, he could appear reserved, but he brought a fierce intelligence to his role at the Lodge and steered it back closer to its original mission under Amy Buller. Living in London, his visits were less frequent than those of the Andersons, which meant that the staff did not him know as well. He was almost as connected in high places as Eric, but more inclined to let his hair down anecdotally. Informal meetings with him were invariably spiced with refreshing political gossip.

Above any trustee were the Visitor and the Patron. When I arrived at the Lodge Princess Margaret was our Visitor and The Queen Mother our Patron. Both died early in 2002. The Visitor's role, fortunately not invoked in my time, was to adjudicate any appeal that might result from a conflict between the Principal and the Chairman. I thought that an Appeal Court judge might be appropriate, besides which it seemed a bit greedy to have two senior royals at the helm. Sir John Laws accepted the post. Regarded as having one of the keenest minds in the judiciary, he and his wife Sophie never declined an invitation to the Lodge. John gave the first Cumberland Lodge Annual Lecture, speaking with extraordinary erudition about Religion, Law and Authority. Normally he was the wittiest of men and I promised the invited audience that they were in for a medley of jokes. It was a brilliant lecture but as dry as a bone. John and Sophie became good friends. Indeed, in 2014 both they and we planned visits within a few weeks of each other to the isolated South Atlantic island of St Helena, conspiratorially comparing notes about this neglected and fascinating outpost of empire.

The Queen Mother spent most weekends at Royal Lodge, walking distance from our Lodge. It was in her time painted pink, and I mentioned to her on one occasion that pink was the traditional colour to indicate a Jacobite affiliation in Scotland. 'Well. I am a Jacobite!' she replied. I thought perhaps she should not say this too loudly if her daughter was close by, being monarch by virtue of Hanoverian descent. We met the Queen Mother on several occasions in the last year of her life. She was by now 100 years old, but lively and fun. When foot and mouth disease threatened to close the Great Park, thus our business at the Lodge, she told me not to worry. 'I will have a word if it comes to it.'

One weekend in December 2001, when she was due to come to Cumberland Lodge for a Christmas drink, she became unwell. She never came again and died the following March. She had done more to make the modern concept of the Lodge possible than any other person and it owes its being to her commitment and influence. I attended her funeral at Westminster Abbey. Guests were instructed not to bring their spouses or partners. I asked the longest serving member of staff, Jean Fielder, a senior housekeeper, to accompany me. We were seated in the front row of the nave, privileged participants in a moving farewell.

Her Majesty The Queen agreed to succeed her mother as Patron, a singular honour as she had made it clear that the patronages of her mother and sister would be given largely to younger members of the Royal Family. She came to the Lodge almost every year I was there, usually on a Sunday morning to meet a few invited guests, but sometimes for private family events, a christening or wake. I would always be on hand. I will never forget the look on the faces of four students who were slouching in the Tapestry Hall one morning when I walked through with The Queen. 'Would you like to meet Her Majesty?' I asked. They liked, and leapt to their feet. Once she had left the Lodge a few minutes later, they all whipped out their mobile 'phones. 'Mum!' I heard one say. 'I've just met the Queen.... No, really, Mum... Mum, honestly, I'm telling the truth!'

Student groups visited the Lodge throughout the year. When this first began in 1947, they were exclusively from the colleges of London University. Indeed, I was able to restore an arrangement with the English department of University College which had lapsed many years earlier because some students had flown the Red Flag on the Queen Mother's birthday. Now departments of many other universities came regularly, including Cambridge, Kingston, Southampton, Warwick and the West of England. They were free to devise their own programmes, but we encouraged them to include at least one session reflecting on the societal and moral nature of their discipline. This was sometimes referred to as the St Catharine's session. I enjoyed these visitors hugely and was always surprised at how well behaved most of them were. In over twelve years I never once saw any graffiti or wilful misuse of the premises. Yes, some students inevitably drank too much: Jane and her team would sometimes have to take a room out of commission while they cleaned up vomit or replaced soiled bed linen. On a few occasions I had to get out of bed in the middle of the night to answer the night porter's plea for assistance as he cajoled boisterous young people to make less noise with their music or, more alarmingly, dealt with sudden illness. In compensation, far outweighing the misdemeanours and crises, were my countless conversations over the years with some of the brightest or most interesting young men and women of their generation. Any fears I might have had bottled up about the future of humanity were generally allayed by their optimism and determination to make a better fist of the world than we had done.

On Sunday mornings guests staying at Cumberland Lodge could, if they passed a police security check, attend Matins at Royal Chapel. This pretty church alongside Royal Lodge serves the residents of the Park, but it is also where The Queen and her family worship when they are in Windsor. The Chaplain of the Park for much of our time was John Ovenden. He and his wife Christine were hospitable neighbours as well as loyally interested in the Lodge's activities. John was under strict instructions to give sermons of no more than seven minutes, lest he exhaust the royal patience. His services breezed along and were always entertaining. I may even have had some spiritual enlightenment from time to time. In our first year, The Queen tended to play second fiddle to her mother, sometimes tapping her fingers on the bonnet of her car as she waited for the Queen Mum to stop talking. After her mother's death, however, The Queen stepped forward and, as our new Patron, invariably spent time with our students or whoever was resident at the Lodge that weekend. Sometimes she was assisted by Prince Philip or by the Duke of York, who moved into Royal Lodge after his grandmother died. My job at such moments, or that of my colleagues, was to ensure that the royals were not crowded out, that conversations were brisk, and that there were no photographs. Only once did I have a security scare. An over-enthusiastic art student thrust her portfolio of pictures into The Queen's hands, expressing hope that she would enjoy them; the royal protection officers were not amused. On better occasions, I could see how much The Queen enjoyed these encounters with young people. She could even find them useful, as when she chatted to members of Birmingham University's Centre for Russian and East European Studies about the forthcoming visit to London of President Putin. She was doing her homework.

Another royal connection came our way only after a lot of preparatory work. Cumberland Lodge became the host institution for the annual Royal Collection summer school. Curators, gallery managers, art dealers – anyone involved with art collections of the highest quality from anywhere in the world – would assemble by invitation for a two-week gathering at the Lodge. They were given private tours of royal palaces and residences, accompanied by leading authorities on the art and furniture they were seeing. We had to be very flexible with timings as trips to London and elsewhere often ran over schedule, but they were among the friendliest and most scholarly gatherings I have ever witnessed. We negotiated our own loans from the Royal Collection and Arts Council England, and I felt that we provided an excellent ambiance for these events. From late night conversations with delegates I learned more than I could ever have expected about national art collections from Mexico to Mongolia.

One of the happiest annual events was also the longest established, going back to 1947. As our final activity of the year, fifty overseas students would come for a celebratory weekend. The idea was to give them a taste of a British Christmas. We sought permission each year from Philip Everett, the Deputy Ranger, to take them by coach through parts of the Park that were normally closed off, with me acting as a rather facetious tour guide. They explored Windsor Castle, then returned for a full-blown Christmas dinner, at which Father Christmas himself would appear, bearing a remarkable resemblance to Robert the chef. A poet or actor would take part. If our intrepid thespian friends, Alison Skilbeck, who I had known since Rafter Player days, and her husband Tim Hardy, were in residence we knew we would have a sophisticated evening of seasonal fun, though contributions of the students themselves, performing a song, dance, poem or recitation from their national culture, were every bit as delightful. On Sunday morning we would always have a moving observance, led by a Christian minister but designed to speak to students of all faiths or none.

In addition to university students, the Lodge played host through the years to many medical groups, brought by their deaneries to discuss the social rather than medical aspects of doctoring. Then there were the lawyers. Each of the four Inns of Court visited, Gray's Inn once a year, Inner Temple and Lincoln's Inn twice, and Middle Temple three times. I made many friends among these witty and clever people. The quality of discussion was superb, with Inner Temple always arranging a panel debate for the whole of a Saturday morning. It should have been broadcast nationally. To hear, just a stone's throw from our house, speakers of the calibre of Cardinal Cormac Murphy-O'Connor or Elizabeth Butler-Sloss talking about ethical dilemmas facing practising lawyers, never failed to excite me.

As for the advocacy sessions, they nurtured not just forensic talent among the trainee barristers, being tutored by some of the most eminent judges and QCs in the land, but also their acting skills. One day I took The Queen and Prince Philip to hear part of a mock trial. The case was Regina on behalf of Goldilocks versus the Three Bears, perhaps the only occasion on record when Regina in person heard evidence being put forward in her name. We left before the end, but as we did so The Queen asked to be kept informed of the verdict.

The programme of talks and conferences we presented, latterly under Owen's expert leadership, never ceased to amaze me. They were thoroughly researched so that, whatever the topic, we knew we had the best speakers in the field. From the time I began at the Lodge, inheriting a conference asking whether architects mattered, to the time I left, I felt that these in-depth gatherings made a measurable difference in every sector they covered. I can cite practical examples of this. Because of the Lodge's conference on 'Migrant Health', for instance, a new policy was adopted by the National Health Service towards special illnesses that black and Asian people were more prone to contract. A conference marking thirty years since HIV-AIDS had been identified proposed a strategy for dealing with the pandemic over the next forty years. 'The Meaning of Museums', attended by some of the country's foremost directors of national collections, asserted their responsibility for conservation as much as for public access. Government pressure to popularise museums with dinosaur exhibitions were all well and good, but was not the protection of historic artefacts just as important? I was taken straight back to the *Lost Heritage* symposium I had organised at the Africa Centre in 1981.

Once a year we held a conference with the police. A standing committee met several times in the preceding months to choose topics and propose speakers. For much of my period Sir Norman Bettison chaired this, shrewdly and tactfully. I always thought that an ideal moment for professional criminals to go about their business would be during these conferences, for up to a third of the nation's Chief Constables might be found at Cumberland Lodge. We examined police responses to domestic abuse, drug trafficking, online pornography, restorative justice and many other subjects, with all ranks of the force present, along with relevant people from charities and local authorities. Theresa May, as Home Secretary, spoke to delegates the year that the concept of elected police and crime commissioners was being introduced. Her audience was sceptical, many believing that it would mean an unnecessary tier of extra bureaucracy. Asked what a typical police and crime commissioner would do at 9 a.m. on a Monday morning, Mrs May hesitated. 'Attend meetings, I suppose,' was her leaden answer. Even she had the grace to laugh, adding, 'That's not a very good reply, is it?'

What Mrs May, in her later incarnation as Prime Minister, would have made of our series of conferences on the European Union I am not sure. These were the brainchild of my spirited colleague Jutta Huesmann, a German who passionately felt that her generation was obliged to carry a millstone labelled 'second world war' round its neck though it was not personally implicated. The EU had kept the peace in Europe for fifty years. One of the issues we examined was whether there was a common European culture, spanning Scandinavia to Greece, with a shared Christian heritage being the glue that held it together. If this was so, what place would Muslim populations have in an expanded Union, perhaps including Turkey? Did geography or democracy define the EU and if the latter might not New Zealand have a better claim to belong than Hungary? These were stimulating conferences intellectually, but they also stimulated a right wing political faction to camp outside the grounds of the Lodge, regaling us over Tannoys with accusations that we were traitors to the Queen in her own property. Eventually this group moved off to Windsor town where they burned the EU flag outside the Castle.

Sometimes we explored lighter or more local topics. We provided many opportunities to examine the history of the Lodge and the Park. 'Art in the Park' took participants around the monuments and statuary within the Great Park itself. The sculptor Philip Jackson enthrallingly explained how he had created both the equestrian statue of The Queen nearby and his statue of her mother overlooking the Mall in London. In the Savill and the Valley Gardens, Windsor Great Park has two national horticultural collections. We ran a slightly subversive conference on why the English love gardening, with the Guerrilla Gardener coming out of hiding to explain his moonlit plantings in abandoned rail sidings and at urban roundabouts.

The Lodge is a Christian foundation, though this has been interpreted in what we would mischievously describe as a very catholic way. Amy Buller blamed the lure of fascism partly on the loss of religion or a moral compass in Germany. I saw a danger in the Lodge appearing to be a latter-day Moral Rearmament centre, but I ensured that discussion of religious and spiritual values was a continuous part of our discourse. The Lodge's own chapel was little used when I arrived, but I reinstated staff services and broadened them to permit our neighbours living alongside to take part. I rejected the view that religion was *passé* out of personal conviction as much as an obligation to our founder's mission. Over coffee with Cardinal Murphy-O'Connor, as he waited to join the Inner Temple debate, a possibility was raised of us testing through one of our events the age-old religious paradox of whether a just war is a valid or contradictory concept. Murphy-O'Connor's conclave colleague Cardinal Arinze had raised the same point on a visit to the Lodge some time earlier. When Owen arrived, I set him to work on the idea as his first project. With his background as a philosopher he pulled it off magnificently – though I am still not sure what the answer is to the mighty question.

I often called in favours from my work in literature over the preceding years. Many poets came to give readings, among them two Poet Laureates, Andrew Motion and Carol Ann Duffy. I had platform conversations with Louis de Bernières, Antonia Fraser, P. D. James, and many other writers, which led me in time to do the same for the Windsor Festival, with whom we came to work as partners. We had a major conference on post-colonial memoirs and another to mark the 150th anniversary of Rabindranath Tagore's birth. Not long after I left the Lodge a handsome volume was published of the best literary papers delivered there, *Discourses of Empire and Commonwealth*, edited by me and my Australian colleague, Sandra Robinson (39), with whom I worked the whole time I was at the Lodge.

To raise our profile locally, I started a series of Cumberland Conversations, which soon played to overflowing audiences and hugely helped to cement a relationship between the Lodge and the wider community. The first of these was given by Michael Mayne, one of the great religious persons of my lifetime, and later guests included Sir Roger Bannister, a life fellow of the Lodge, and the actress Virginia McKenna. I introduced Roger to our son Alex, who was then sixteen, describing him in advance as the greatest British athlete of all time. Alex was puzzled as to how this could be, seeing before him an amiable but stooped old man with a stick. As for Virginia, I disgraced myself in our public conversation by clumsily rhapsodizing about her beauty, when all she wanted to talk about was saving lions.

I have referred to our neighbours. There was a line of grace and favour cottages close by the Lodge, lived in by former employees of the Royal Household or others close to the crown. To my shock I discovered when we moved in that most of them knew nothing about the Lodge and in one case, though he had lived alongside it for more than a dozen years, had never set foot within it. Helen and I set about getting to know these residents and they all became friends. Helen used regularly to read to Lady Mary Clayton, a cousin of the Queen, whose taste in books often lay in royal memoirs. She would pass incisive comments, born from personal memories, about 'David and Wallis', or whomever was being read about. Then there was Elizabeth Pearce, who had been secretary to Lord Moore, the Queen's Private Secretary. She was acerbic about almost everyone but kind underneath. Gordon Franklin, who had headed personnel at Buckingham Place, and his wife Gill were always keen to meet our foreign students.

Like an elder statesman to them all was Walter James, who had been Principal of the Lodge before Lord Vaizey and editor of *The Times Educational Supplement* before that. His much younger wife Jocelyn died not long after our arrival, but his daughter Sophie and his grandson lived nearby. Walter was still driving at 102. He had a sharp mind and a devout soul. At chapel services he alone would kneel as the Host was raised and we younger mortals looked on. On his 90th, 95th and 100th birthdays we gave celebratory lunches, the guests including some of the young journalists such as Simon Jenkins whom Walter had once trained. Our Scottish friend Juliet Clough was among them, as coincidentally it transpired that she was Sophie's godmother as well as our Alex's. On the day Walter turned 100 the whole staff turned out to clap him into the building. Only shortly before he had been *chevalier d'honneur* at the marriage in the Royal Chapel of the music critic Patrick Carnegie and the opera singer Jill Gomez, now Earl and Countess of Northesk. I was invited to give a speech at the reception after, but I was eclipsed by Walter's *debonnaire* charm and Patrick's tartan trews.

No one memory encapsulates our life at Cumberland Lodge. If pushed to it, however, I would cite the 60th anniversary celebrations of the Foundation in 2007 as epitomising the best of our years there. It seemed that everyone wanted to join in, including the Great Park community and the Royal Chapel congregation, for a special service arranged by John Ovenden, at which The Queen was present. I wrote a Cumberland Lodge prayer for the occasion and my old friend Lawrence Sail a sonnet, 'Cumberland Lodge At Sixty'.

> We keep the score in years
> though knowing perfectly well
> that, for the spirit to flourish,
> there always must be a place
> set back from history, a building
> listed grade one for silence,
> or for speech which discounts the tallies
> of time that abrade our dreams.
>
> All down the grand avenue
> of twenty-two frayed limes
> stand the shadows and angles
> of other possible trees,
> fluttering the broad discourse
> of their countless heart-shaped leaves. (40)

We moved out of Groom's House for our last five years – it was needed for bedrooms and seminar rooms to accommodate the Lodge's growing business. Marina Vaizey, John Vaizey's widow, opened the refurbished building. Art critic of *The Observer*, Lady Vaizey had been responsible in her husband's era for much of the art collection at the Lodge. I was able to do a deal with the Arts Council replenishing this with modern British masterpieces by David Hockney and others. We started regular exhibitions on the ground floor of the Lodge and sometimes in the grounds outside. Two of these displayed work from the Royal School of Needlework, seldom seen publicly. I escorted The Queen round them and she commented that The Lord Chancellor's Purse, in which her Speech is placed at the State Opening of Parliament, and which had been loaned to us, was difficult to manipulate. After a word in the right place, I believe it was adjusted. I much enjoyed working with Christopher Mann and the College of Arms on an exhibition about heraldry. The Duke of Norfolk opened this and regaled us with excellent, if slightly indiscreet stories. The Garter King of Arms allowed us to show the dress he would be required to don if called upon to proclaim a new monarch.

I loved every moment in Windsor. It was hard, looking out from our new home in Studio Cottage over the surrounding garden and fields towards a burgeoning vineyard, not to exclaim each time on how lucky we were to be in such a place. Studio Cottage had been lived in before us by Sir John Johnston, a close friend of royalty and the last wielder of the blue pencil censoring drama on behalf of the Lord Chamberlain. When Johnnie died, we had asked The Queen if the Lodge could take it over. She agreed and after it had been redecorated according to the guidance of a specialist in period design, Will Hawkes, she and Prince Philip came to see the result. Legend had it that George III, in his years of mental illness, had used it for his water colouring and drawing – hence its name. It certainly had a big room with a cupola to let in masses of natural light, but we were never able to verify the tale.

In addition to our dog Ben and our cat Tim, who often walked together last thing at night in the field behind the house, we also kept chickens. Daisy, Maisie, Gertie and Germaine Greer lived in a Buckingham Palace of chicken runs to protect them from foxes, nearly thirty of which were culled each month in the Park. When Daisy died, Alex went to dispose of her in some undergrowth nearby. As always happened, for nothing escapes their eyes, a Park gamekeeper popped up. Alex explained what he was doing and how sad his family was at the chicken's demise. The gamekeeper was a philosopher, saying in his Berkshire burr, 'Where you've got livestock, you've also got deadstock'.

Certain commitments in the community accrued to the role of Principal. A short walk away stood the Royal School, the only school in the country entitled to describe itself as 'crown aided'. A state school of only a hundred children, it went through various ups and downs while I served on its governing body, but it came right in the end. I took over from John Ovenden as Chairman for a few years. I was also President of the Windsor branch of the Workers Educational Association. I learned much from its excellent one-day conferences and, as often as I could, took part in their committee meetings because they were both instructive and convivial. Then there was Windsor Castle itself, where we sometimes worked on joint events with St George's House, a foundation not unlike our own.

In 2012 The Queen made me a Lieutenant of the Royal Victorian Order, an honour within her personal gift. I was invested at Windsor Castle by the Princess Royal, who a few months earlier had given our tenth annual lecture. She had spoken reflectively on three topics: her mother's Diamond Jubilee as monarch, the Olympic Games and the Paralympics, all of which had occurred that year. She was tender in her tribute to her parents. The big surprise, however, was her appreciation of Ken Livingstone, whom she described as the unsung hero of the Olympics. Princess Anne's ability to speak well without notes is legendary. I discovered that it involved ignoring my notes too, which I had offered as briefing. Her superb lecture and the dinner that followed were her seventh engagement of the day, but she arrived by helicopter impeccably on time and fully prepared, a model of professionalism.

John Ovenden had handed over the chaplaincy to Martin Poll, whom Helen helped to appoint, and Philip Everett was preparing to pass on the Deputy Rangership to Paul Sedgewick. It was time for us to move on too. We left Cumberland Lodge at the end of March 2013. Shortly before we did, Her Majesty and the Duke of Edinburgh came to bid us farewell. I had read in the press that she was under the weather and would forego the annual Commonwealth Observance in Westminster

Abbey the next day. When her detective rang a few hours before she was due, I assumed it was to say that neither she nor the Duke would be coming. Instead I was told that they were determined still to be with us. Helen and I were deeply touched. My brother Peter had died of cancer three days before. I was able to pass on The Queen's commiserations to Peta, my sister-in-law. Martin Newlan took a photograph of Helen and me, Isabella, her partner Nic, and Alex, standing with the royal couple. I am sure it will be a family heirloom.

*

I managed to keep up a few external commitments while working in Windsor. In 2003 I was elected President of English PEN. My predecessor Victoria Glendinning twisted my arm to stand. I was not at all sure it was the right thing to do because all those who had previously been in the post had been distinguished authors, from John Galsworthy onwards. I had been a member of PEN for a few years and had dealings with it when I was at the Arts Council. P. D. James had unflatteringly described it as a society for distressed gentlefolk. I was more positive than that, but I recognised that it had a rather excluding side to it. By the time I became President it had professionalised itself, with a paid director and thus an annual subsidy from the Arts Council. All on the surface boded well.

What I had not reckoned on was the continuing discontent that rumbled underneath. It was an unhappy organisation. I knew that to carry credibility I must have a respected author working alongside me, and so created the post of Deputy President. Lisa Appignanesi took this on, brilliantly campaigning for the right to offend as a necessary hallmark of free expression. I had an excellent committee to work with and in Jonathan Heawood an outstandingly competent Director. There was, however, a faction still strongly opposed to the changes that had taken place before my time. I was publicly described by the crime writer and journalist Joan Smith as a Stalinist. I covertly rather enjoyed the soubriquet, but it was not comfortable to be denounced in Politburo language. On one occasion, at a PEN reception in 2005, I introduced myself to the Russian dissident writer Anna Politkovskaya, who was visiting London from Moscow. Joan was talking to her as I approached and cut me dead so conspicuously that Anna picked up on it and asked me discreetly what was wrong between us. The tale was too long to tell there and then, so I missed my chance as Anna, tragically, was assassinated the following year.

Isabella graduated from Falmouth College of Arts in 2004, but her graduation day, though gloriously sunny, was marred for me by an article by Michael White in *The Guardian* that morning predicting blood on the carpet at the English PEN annual general meeting the following week. I spent much of what should have been a celebratory weekend addressing White's melodramatic representations. I believe it may in the end have marked a turning point for the organisation, for the meeting went well. It was as though PEN members had peered into an abyss and not liked what lay below. The civil war came to a close and for the rest of my period of office, which was extended by a year, we were able to concentrate on our work, supporting writers who had fallen foul of tyrannical regimes, espousing free expression, running a busy programme of talks and publications, and advocating translation. I went to the International PEN Congresses in Tromsø in 2004 and in Dakar in 2007, revelling in the camaraderie.

I must highlight one of English PEN's campaigns on behalf of an unjustly incarcerated writer. Though it predated my term as President, it affected Helen and me personally. Our friendship with the Malawian poet Jack Mapanje went back many years. In 1987, on the orders of President Hastings Banda, Jack was imprisoned without charge. It took nearly four years of international agitation on his behalf, and a threat by the British government to cut off development aid to Malawi, to secure his release. Antonia Fraser, President of English PEN at the time, and her husband Harold Pinter, spearheaded the protests. My own role in these was marginal. On his release Jack learned that if he stayed in Malawi he would be 'accidentalised' – i.e., eliminated. He came to England for refuge, accompanied by his wife Mercy and his three children. His friend, the South African writer Landeg White, who was living nearby, arranged for the family to settle in York. They spent their first Christmas in England with us. Five years later, while attached to the Open University for a few weeks, Jack lived in our attic, beginning there his classic prison memoir *And Crocodiles are Hungry at Night* (41). Jack was born one month to the day after me and so occasionally refers to me as his senior brother. The truth is the other way round, for he has talent and a degree of humility to which I can only aspire. We have been to both his daughters' weddings, first in Uganda and second in St. Lucia, and treasure memories of his son Lika and our son kicking a football round our garden when they were lads. Of such is life really made.

*

As we drove away from Windsor Great Park on Maundy Thursday 2013, leaving my colleagues to an Easter celebration. Helen and I were rather quiet. It was an epic moment. We wondered about the future. It seemed that our careers were over. Our children were launched on their lives. We were moving to a house in Kennington, where we knew no one.

The future is another country. What we have both discovered is that the best of life lies within ourselves. We are fortunate to have kept our health, so far, to have loving children, so far, to like our son-out-law very much, and to feel we made the right choice, against much advice, by moving into London, where we have friendly people living on either side of us. It is an ethnically diverse area where every day you overhear many languages. The occasional gunshot, linked to the drug dealing we know goes on nearby, does not deter us from loving both our house, unsuitable though we are told it is because of its many stairs, and our 'Georgian strip' of a garden. Nic has designed and erected an award-winning studio for Helen, and I sit at a vast desk, which the trustees of Cumberland Lodge gave me when I left, looking towards Kennington Park. What's not to like, even though Ben and Tim and the chickens have all passed on?

For four years, at the invitation of Michael Caine's widow, Baroness Nicholson, I worked part time for the Iraq Britain Business Council, trying to establish some educational links between Britain and Iraq. I went three times to Iraq, always under intense security. It is a great country, historically. With its oil wealth it may be again. I found it hard to clinch any arrangement because decision making becomes paralysed by the constant rotation of Iraqi ministers, all nervous of responsibility and, alas, many of them more dedicated to self-interest than to national development. Emma Nicholson's staunch determination never wavers. I believe she should be given the Nobel Peace Prize for her work on health and education in Iraq.

In 2012 Ralph Waller, a trustee of Cumberland Lodge and Principal of Harris Manchester College at Oxford, inducted me as an Honorary Fellow, ensuring that I had a continuing university affiliation. This privilege came just before I left the Lodge. From the day I gave up my post at Stirling to now I have always had a university link, allowing me access to research facilities and camaraderie with fellow academics. The new University of Gibraltar, for example, invited me to give a lecture in 2017 to mark its first award of a Commonwealth Scholarship. There can be no more beautifully sited campus in the world, looking across to Spain in one direction, the Atlas Mountains in another, with the Rock itself just behind. A daunting experience, as the lecture was given before the Governor and Chief Minister of Gibraltar, it led to a continuing link with this enterprising institution. I value, too, my association with Bath Spa University, where membership of their Ethics Panel provides hours of stimulating debate each year on matters to do with research and teaching standards.

I continue to have many voluntary commitments, including chairing the board of *The Annual Register of World Events*, which has been published every year since Edmund Burke founded it in 1758. I maintain my long association with Commonwealth Scholars, chairing its Support Group. In this I am tactfully prompted by the indefatigable Peter Williams, a Commonwealth guru if ever there was one. I am a trustee of the Council for Education in the Commonwealth, of the Stephen Spender Trust, and of the Caine Prize for African Writing. I also co-chair the Events Committee of the English-Speaking Union.

I have had special pleasure from my connection with Border Crossings, a theatre company punching well above its financial weight under the inspiringly energetic leadership of Michael Walling. We work in most art forms – plays, film, art, debate – but the jewel in our crown is a biennial festival in London called *Origins*, which focuses on indigenous cultures: Aboriginal, Amazonian, Inuit, Maori, Sámi.

In 2014 I judged the Man Booker Prize. In the twenty years since I had previously been on a Booker jury, I kept in touch with friends who ran it. In 2007 I happened to be talking to Doris Lessing at the award ceremony in London when we were called into dinner. I offered my arm to the 88 year old writer, who had only a few days earlier been named as winner of the Nobel Prize for Literature. We entered the Guildhall together. As we did so there was a huge burst of clapping. I felt so proud escorting Doris at that moment.

Judging the prize again was in most respects a happier experience than two decades before, though the number of entries was greater and choice even more complex. A. C. Grayling chaired the jury, and our deliberations were more thorough. Towards the end of the process, however, the director of the prize, Ion Trewin, fell ill and had to withdraw. His death the following year left the literary world deeply bereaved. We selected Richard Flanagan's novel *The Narrow Road to the Deep North* (42) as the winner. Flanagan's acceptance speech was the best of its kind I have ever heard.

Linked only by name, Michael Caine created the Russian Booker Prize. Its aim each year for a quarter of a century has been to name the best novel in the Russian language. I have been an informal adviser to the Prize, which is shrewdly run by the distinguished scholar of English literature, Igor Shaitanov. It has taken me to Moscow several times, sometimes in the company of Michael's widow, Emma. As I write, the prize is being 'rested' for want of sponsorship. President Putin has made it illegal to accept Russian diasporic funding. He seems peculiarly nervous of it and has set up his own fiction award in an attempt to neutralise it.

Helen and I continue to travel. Since leaving Windsor we have been in every continent except Antarctica, which is a pity because one of our best conferences at Cumberland Lodge focused on how the Antarctic Treaty, drawn up in 1961 between the major nations working there, could be a model for all treaty making. We have been in Australia to celebrate the 80th birthday of our friend, the poet Chris Wallace-Crabbe. There I discovered that his partner, Kristin Headlam, one of Australia's best portrait painters, had painted me from a photograph. I asked her to touch up the thinning hair, but she declined to do so for mate's rates. I forgave her and the picture is now in our living room. I have paid a second visit to Myanmar, this time with Helen, a country embedded in my family history. We went on the last surviving Royal Mail Ship in the world to Saint Helena, five days out from Cape Town and five days back. Of our many other trips, those to Ethiopia and Iran stand out, not just for their histories, cultures, and natural beauty, but because of the warmth of friendship we met in both countries. As I write, because of Covid-19, foreign travel is almost an extinct species, but its time will come again.

Covid-19 also threatens our pleasure in art and theatre, but as both go back to the beginnings of civilisation

– indeed, define it – I know they will return too. We can walk home from many of the great playhouses and galleries, and hardly a month goes by without the opening in London of a major retrospective art exhibition. How lucky we were to be guests of David Cohen and Jillian Barker at a private showing of the National Gallery's exhibition of Leonardo da Vinci's paintings. At one point in the evening we had a whole room to ourselves, yet this was an event to which even royalty could not always get admission. We see as many exhibitions as we can, but some escape us.

As for theatre, it has been an abiding passion ever since an aunt took me to see *The Happiest Days of Your Life* in Edinburgh when I was a boy. My father used to take us at Christmas to the Victoria Palace to see the Crazy Gang – they appealed to his sense of humour whatever the rest of us thought. Their shows were wholly unsuitable for innocent children, but I adored the crudeness and warmth. Perhaps they gave me my taste for the lowbrow as much as the highbrow. I am lucky to have seen great comics such as Ken Dodd, Frankie Howerd and Max Wall. In my youth I saw the cream of classical actors, John Gielgud and Laurence Olivier, Edith Evans, Sybil Thorndike and Flora Robson, and from other countries Marie Bell, Vittorio Gassman, Robert Hirsch and Aspasia Papathanasiou. I feel I have lived my life alongside Judi Dench, Ian McKellen, Maggie Smith, Peter Hall and Trevor Nunn, the National Theatre and Royal Shakespeare Company. I am sometimes asked by friends who know about my obsession what I consider the greatest performance I ever saw. Perhaps it was Peggy Ashcroft as Queen Margaret in *The Wars of the Roses*. Then I re-wind and think of the most under-recognised major actor in the country, Barbara Jefford, essaying Shakespeare's Cleopatra and Dryden's Cleopatra on the same day at the Theatre Royal in Glasgow, John Kani in *Sizwe Bansi is Dead* in Stirling, Ian Holm's King Lear, Glenda Jackson's King Lear, Mark Rylance in almost anything. I spend a lot of time in fringe theatres seeking out lost plays from other eras or new dramatists whose time is to come. I once flew to Belfast just to see a Beckett triple bill hardly more than an hour in length. I have seen productions dismissed by friends as 'crap', plays that ran out of steam before the interval, actors in the nude for no good reason, directors showing off, productions that have left me covered in fake blood or simulated ordure. Never once have I regretted being there or considered walking out. My next task is to bring all these reflections together in a book. It will also explain why I think opera may be the greatest of all the arts.

We are much in touch with Colin, Isabella and Nic, Alex and Peter's widow, Peta, with Helen's brother Bryan and his daughters and grandchildren. Sustained by our families, we look back with gratitude and forward with optimism. I am aware of living in an age of frighteningly second-rate and overweening political leaders, but they and their kind cannot last forever. Humankind has an instinct for survival and will find a way of coping with pandemics, climate change, and economic downturns, because the alternatives are disintegration and despair. I feel I have spent my whole life in one long conversation; only the settings have changed. Sometimes it has been within my family, or at school, or in universities, or in the cherished institutions in which I have been privileged to work. The participants have been various, from the highest to the humblest. But it has been the same continuing conversation and it has never flagged.

I take my cue from our venerable friend, Nirad Chaudhuri. With Hugo Brunner, the Lord Lieutenant of Oxfordshire, Helen and I hosted a luncheon for him on 23rd November 1997, his 100th birthday. At the end of his great *Autobiography of an Unknown Indian*, he writes:

Today, borne on a great flood of faith, hope, and joy in the midst of infinite degradation, I feel that I shall be content to be nothing for ever after death in the ecstasy of having lived and been alive for a moment. I have made the discovery that the last act is glorious however squalid the play may be in all the rest. (43)

I share this ecstasy, though the play for me has never been squalid. I look back in gratitude and surprise at both its glad and sorry hours. Now in the fifth act, I put my trust in an infinite epilogue, to be known only after the curtain has fallen.

***

ACKNOWLEDGEMENTS

I would like to be able to write that everyone mentioned in this book has been helpful in the writing of it, if only because our paths once crossed. It would, however, be stretching it a bit to thank Elizabeth I or Clement Attlee. There are a few individuals who I have not much enjoyed encountering in my career, but they are not worth dwelling upon, for they did not linger. Like everyone, I have relied all my life on the kindness of an infinite number of strangers. I have been fortunate to have had lifelong friends, supportive colleagues and inspiring teachers, many of whom I have not mentioned but without whom I could not have prospered. I have been entrusted with the good will of many authors and public figures, but the comradeship of young people, especially students, has probably meant the most to me. I express my gratitude to everyone who has received an email or telephone call from me in the past few months as I checked a fact or verified my faltering anecdotal memory. The support of Chip Martin, who had the idea for this book many years ago and who has overseen its arrival, is inestimable.

Without Isabella, Nic, Alex, Colin, Peta and above all Helen, *In Glad or Sorry Hours* would have been far more sorrowful and far less glad. They embody everything that most matters to me.

Alastair Niven, 4 August 2020

NOTES

1. Charles L. Warr, *The Glimmering Landscape*, London: Hodder and Stoughton, 1960, 71-72

2. H. J. C. Grierson, Preface, Alexander William Mair, *Poems*, Edinburgh: Oliver and Boyd, 1929, 10

3. 'Song Before Sunrise (After Heine)', Mair, *op.cit.*, 59

4. Hilaire Belloc, 'Rebecca, Who Slammed Doors For Fun And Perished Miserably', *Cautionary Tales for Children*, London: Eveleigh Nash, 1907

5. Euripides, trans. Philip Vellacott, *Alcestis*, Harmondsworth: Penguin, 1953, closing lines

6. William Shakespeare, *The Winter's Tale*, II, i

7. Shakespeare, *Twelfth Night*, I, i

8. Shakespeare, *The Tempest*, II, i

9. The Robbins Report: Higher Education Report of the Committee appointed by the Prime Minister under the Chairmanship of Lord Robbins, 1961-63

10. Alastair Niven, *D. H. Lawrence: The Novels*, Cambridge: Cambridge University Press, 1978. Joined two years later by *D. H. Lawrence: The Writer and his Work – A Writers and Their Work Special*, Harlow: Longman, 1980

11. Niven, *The Yoke of Pity: The Fictional Writings of Mulk Raj Anand*, New Delhi: Arnold Heinemann, 1978

12. Niven, *Truth Within Fiction*, Calcutta: Writers Workshop, 1987

13. E. G. Allingham, *A Romance of the Rostrum – Being the business life of Henry Stevens and the history of Thirty-eight King Street, together with some account of famous sales held there during the last hundred years.* London: H. F. and G. Witherby, 1924

14. Africa Centre Annual Report, 1979

15. *Lost Heritage: The Question of the Return of Cultural Property*, Report of the Symposium Held in London 1981, London: Commonwealth Arts Association and Africa Centre, 1981, 26

16. Niven (ed.), *Under Another Sky*: The Commonwealth Poetry Prize Anthology, Manchester: Carcanet, 1987; Grace Nichols, 'Epilogue', *I is a long memoried woman*, London: Karnak House, 1983

17. Peter Porter, 'The Last of England', *The Last of England*, Oxford, O.U.P., 1971

18. Eric Ashby, *Community of Universities: An informal portrait of the Association of Commonwealth Universities 1913-1963*, Cambridge: C.U.P., for the A.C.U., 1963

19. Hugh W. Springer, in collaboration with Niven, *The Commonwealth of Universities: The Story of the Association of Commonwealth Universities, 1963-1988*, London: Association of Commonwealth Universities, 1988

20. Ralph Heintzman, editor, *Tom Symons: A Canadian Life*, Ottawa, University of Ottawa Press, 2011, Niven, 'Tom Symons and the Commonwealth', 225-238

21. *The Glory of the Garden: The Development of the Arts in England, a Strategy for a Decade*, London: Arts Council of Great Britain, 1984

22. Lawrence Sail, 'The Cheshire Cat's Grin', *Cross-Currents: Essays*, London: Enitharmon, 2005, 11

23. Thomas Gray, 'Elegy Written in a Country Churchyard', 1751

24. Wilfred Owen, 'Strange Meeting', 1918

25. Shakespeare, *Cymbeline*, IV, ii

26. Gary McKeone and Jane O'Brien, *A Poetry Survey for the Arts Council of England: Key Findings*, 1996

27. Stephen Sondheim (lyrics) and Leonard Bernstein (music), 'Somewhere', *West Side Story*, 1957

28. Salman Rushdie, 'The Empire Writes Back with a Vengeance'. *The Times*, 3 July 1982

29. Jean Echenoz, *Lac*, Paris: Les Éditions de Minuit, 1989

30. Debjani Chatterjee, *Barbed Lines*, Leeds: Yorkshire Arts Circus, 1990

31. Rosemary Hill, *God's Architect: Pugin and the Building of Romantic Britain*, London: Allen Lane, 2007

32. James Kelman, *How Late It Was, How Late*, London: Harvill Secker, 1994

33. Jill Paton Walsh, *Knowledge of Angels*, Cambridge: Green Bay Publications, 1994

34. Violet M. Hughes, *Literature Belongs to Everyone: A Report on Widening Access to Literature*, London: Arts Council of Great Britain, 1991

35. Andrew Sinclair, *Arts and Cultures: The History of the 50 Years of the Arts Council of Great Britain*, London: Sinclair-Stevenson, 1995

36. Bryan Cheyette, *Muriel Spark*, Writers and Their Work, Tavistock: Northcote House in association with the British Council, 2000

37. [no author attributed], *Cumberland Lodge: A Brief History and Guide*, Bognor Regis: Phillimore, 2015

38. E. Amy Buller, *Darkness Over Germany*, London: Longmans, Green and Co., 1943. Republished as *Darkness Over Germany: A Warning from History*, London: Arcadia, 2017

39. Sandra Robinson & Niven, *Discourses of Empire and Commonwealth*, Leiden: Brill Rodopi, 2016

40. Lawrence Sail, 'Cumberland Lodge At Sixty', unpublished
41. Jack Mapanje, *And Crocodiles Are Hungry at Night*, Banbury: Ayebia Clarke, 2011
42. Richard Flanagan, *The Narrow Road to the Deep North*, London: Chatto and Windus, 2014
43. Nirad C. Chaudhuri, *Autobiography of an Unknown Indian*, London: Macmillan, 1951, 515

Pictures, by chapter

1. Mickey, Harold (with our tortoise Mrs Merrifield) and Betty Niven, circa 1960
2. Brothers: Colin, Peter, Alastair, 1984
3. Derek Moore, Prafulla Mohanti, Mulk Raj Anand, Mulk's daughter Susheila, Alex, Alastair, Helen, Isabella, 1986
4. Alastair with Isabella in her Moses basket at the Africa Centre, with Ben Nganda and Murray McCartney, 1981
5. Sydney Chikafa, Jack Mapanje, Alex, Lika Mapanje, 1997
6. Bernardine Evaristo, Andrea Levy, Alastair in New Zealand, 2000
7. Sir Stephen Wall, H.R.H. The Princess Royal, Alastair at Cumberland Lodge, 2012

Isabella, Alastair, Helen, Alex at Buckingham Palace, 2001